Advance Copy

FOR

Toby + Ben

with warm good wishes
and high regards
We appreciate your friendship
over many years.

Peter Megargee Brown.
October 28, 1989

# RASCALS

## THE SELLING OF THE LEGAL PROFESSION

*Peter Megargee Brown*

Published by
BENCHMARK PRESS

Library of Congress Cataloging-in-Publication Data
Brown, Peter Megargee
Rascals: The Selling of the Legal Profession
Includes selected bibliography
Peter Megargee Brown — First Edition
ISBN 0-915011-05-0

1. Lawyers as rascals engaged in crime, greed, perfidy and sloth.
2. Decline of the American law profession.
3. Rise of the Mega Law Firm.
4. History of the legal profession.
5. Separation of the Bar into licensed Counsellors and unlicensed Attorneys.
6. Remedies for legal reform to restore honor and public responsibility.

Library of Congress catalogue #89-061923
Manufactured in the United States of America
Produced by Fred Weidner & Son, Printers, Inc.
This book set in Garamond No. 3 by Partners Composition
Printed and Bound in acid free paper
by Cushing-Malloy, Inc.
Jacket and book design by Daniel J. McClain
This is an Indigo book

Cover jacket sketch elevation for a triumphal arch
at Temple Bar-London-by court architect Inigo Jones
First Edition

To purchase copies directly write or call Benchmark Press
100 Park Avenue, Suite 2606
New York, New York 10017
Telephone 212-599-1631

# CONTENTS

INTRODUCTION 5
*Crime, Greed, Perfidy & Sloth*

PREFACE 9
*"Where Some Rascals Are Taking Our Law Profession"*

PART ONE 11
- *I. The Leaders of the Bar. The New Giant Law Firms* 12
- *II. The Character and Example of Individual Lawyers at the Bar* 21

PART TWO 43
- *III. What Has Happened to the Law Profession?* 44
- *IV. Legal Narcissism, Manners & Morals* 54

PART THREE 61
- *V. Rise of the MegaLawFirm and The American Law Profession in the Year 2000* 62
- *VI. Morals of the Marketplace* 73
- *VII. Lawyers as Thick as Locusts* 82

PART FOUR 88
- *VIII. The Lawyers' Monopoly: The Exclusive Franchise* 89
- *IX. Roots of Law Practice* 94

PART FIVE 97
- *X. Separate the Bar to Save the Profession* 98
- *XI. Restoring Collegiality & Grace: A Sampler* 102
- *XII. Conclusion: What Should Be Done? Twenty Remedies With Some Chance of Working* 106

AUTHOR'S PERSONAL NOTE 110
*Confrontation About the Changing Nature of the Law Profession*

ABOUT THE AUTHOR 121

BIBLIOGRAPHY 122

# I

"Let no young man choosing the law for a calling for a moment yield to the popular belief [that lawyers are necessarily dishonest]—*resolve* to be honest at all events; and if in your judgment you cannot be an honest lawyer, resolve to be honest without being a lawyer. Choose some other occupation, rather than one in the choosing of which you do, in advance, consent to be a knave."

—ABRAHAM LINCOLN

# II

"Something seriously disturbing has been happening to the legal profession."

—SOL M. LINOWITZ, LAWYER AND PUBLIC SERVANT

# III

"As a profession, lawyers do differ from other callings. This is not a fancy conceit, but a cherished tradition, the preservation of which is essential to the lawyer's reverence for his calling."

—MR. JUSTICE LEWIS F. POWELL, JR.
dissenting from the majority view in *Bates v. State Bar of Arizona* that the practice of law is a trade.

# INTRODUCTION

## *Crime, Greed, Perfidy & Sloth*

THE THEME OF THIS BOOK is that the American law profession should be largely free of crime, perfidy, greed and sloth. That is not true today. Too many lawyers treat the practice of law as a trade solely for profit rather than as a profession for service to the public interest.

This shift of view—to making money—impacts harmfully on American society. We need practical reforms to reinvigorate the law profession as a strong cadre for inspiring a better civilization.

I began writing this book seven years ago observing changes of attitude and outlook in the profession which revealed signs of troubles ahead.

There are large numbers of lawyers who are honest and hardworking, not motivated solely by desire for financial gain and self-aggrandizement. However, in this era of widespread greed, hype and self-dealing, there is a significant and growing number of lawyers to whom the making of money has become the prime, if not the sole, object in the law practice.

As a result, essential elements of trust and confidence between client and attorney evaporate, leaving a residue of arms-length pursuit of money for money's sake. Like a cancer, greed is spreading through the legal profession. It must be cut out before it destroys the profession and, in turn, our entire system of justice.

Many of the greedy ones are found today practicing in the large law firms, often called "megaLawFirms", which, in the last dozen years alone, have risen up suddenly, like the skyscrapers which they inhabit. Too often the bottom-line of profit has replaced quality, humanity and integrity of legal services as the primary objective.

I concede there is evidence in other areas of American society of a deteriorating ethic. Sometimes it seems the difference between right and wrong has flown out the window. To talk about right and wrong today often labels the speaker as old hat, reactionary, perhaps even a bit balmy.

The practice of law has not always been self-serving and gross. Until recently there were very few firms with more than fifty lawyers — practically none with over one hundred. The partners and associates all knew each other and the *size* of the firm permitted them to function as a team. They worked hard and made a good living, but virtually none acquired a fortune at the law. An example of excellence in service to the public and to the profession is John J. McCloy, who died on March 11, 1989 at 93, after a dedicated and versatile career at the Bar. There used to be considerable prestige in being an able and respected lawyer, perhaps a notch ahead of the ordinary businessman. This is not so today. Lawyers today are placed, poll after poll, ignominiously at the bottom of the barrel.

Granted, the growth of American corporations since the 1940s has required legal services which are more easily rendered by large firms. But that fact does not justify the greed and selfishness of the new megaLawFirm. Nor does it justify the oppression and abuse of those men and women who give their days and nights, strangely Orwellian, to the big law firms' object of making money.

Many of us forget that lawyers, by their admission to the Bar, receive an exclusive monopoly to practice law. No one else can do so. The use of this monopoly for exalting profits is contrary to the basic concept and spirit of the profession. With the grant of monopoly comes the responsibility to use it for the good of all. Unless this responsibility is fulfilled, our system of justice, of which lawyers are a vital part, is seriously endangered.

In Chapters One and Two, I have included some horror stories to make the reader aware of what is going on — in case the reader does not already know. I have attempted to show as objectively as possible, by first-hand report and insight, what goes on behind the closed doors of a megaLawFirm.

The balance of the book examines the origins and special nature of the law profession, its times of power and glory, its emerging narcissism, egotism, its declining manners and morals, and the sudden rise of the megaLawFirms.

Final Chapters present possible solutions to the dilemma by separating the Bar into licensed "counsellors-at-law" and unlicensed but certified "attorneys-at-law" and other remedies that may have some chance of working to save the profession from demise.

One thing is certain: There is no quick fix. Too many lawyers today by their narrow education, without philosophy, literature or history, are ill prepared for service in what is essentially a humanistic profession.

This is not a snide lawyer-bashing book; nor is it an angry or sour-grapes book. There is no urging here to go backwards to earlier, nostalgic years of practice; rather, the encouragement is for the Bar to recognize its creeping disintegration and equip itself to meet challenges of the future with vigor and success.

Personal experiences I've had for over forty years in the law practice have been, and still are, stimulating and rewarding. To let the reader assess any edge of bias in my viewpoint, first publicly expressed at the American Bar Association Annual Meeting in 1983, I have appended a personal note about my attempted ouster in 1982 by a new management committee of a large Wall Street law firm.

Law is the instrument of justice and lawyers are supposed to be guardians of the law. We must be willing to confront the crisis of a legal profession now spinning out of control.

# PREFACE

## *"Where Some Rascals Are Taking Our Law Profession"— Chief Justice Warren E. Burger, Letter to the Author*

THE LEGAL PROFESSION during the past twelve years reveals disquieting evidence of decline, as these chapters will show. Root causes of the downfall are difficult to grasp because they principally arise out of short-sighted *attitudes* and *perspectives* of a substantial number of lawyers coast to coast.

Best to look directly at what the infliction of these new attitudes and outlooks within the profession has brought to everyday affairs and relationships. This will illuminate the growing problem by exposing, in the following pages, hard facts in the real world.

The mistake repeatedly made is to assume the law profession is just another calling to which the low common denominator applies. We readily employ the flawed notion of relativism to the law profession — with evil and unnecessary consequences, as Mr. Justice Lewis F. Powell, Jr. pointed out in his strong dissent in 1977 in *Bates v. State Bar of Arizona* to the wrongful notion that the practice of law is a trade. The consequences on the law profession of the Supreme Court majority decision have been horrendous.

We should have been paying attention. When United States Attorney General George Wickersham presented his famed Report on crime to the Congress in 1931, he clearly pointed out the essential difference:

"It will not do to say, as has been said so often, that 'lawyers are as honest as those in other callings.' *Much more than a high average of conventional honesty is demanded of those who are to assist the courts in administering and maintaining justice.*"

The difference is crucial to America and — it is the argument of this book — to civilization.

# PART ONE

## *I. The Leaders of the American Bar: The New Giant Law Firms*

## *II. The Character and Example of Individual Lawyers at the Bar*

*"There are theatres of violence, rebellions and uprisings of all sorts, mass hypocrisy and false sincerity fueled by television, and a general decay in courtesy and a decay of decency; but I don't despair."*

—JAMES RESTON

# I

## *The Leaders of the American Bar: The New Giant Law Firms*

THE REVEALING EPISODES in this chapter arise out of the "law practice" of the new giant law firms:

• Example: On Friday, January 23, 1987 at 9:45 a.m., a partner, earning $500,000 a year in a large, high-powered national law firm was sentenced by Federal court Judge Robert Sweet to a year and a day in jail.

A licensed lawyer, he was caught red-handed stealing confidential information from his firm's clients and feeding it to a security fraud ringleader.

The lawyer being sentenced, Ilan Reich, an associate and finally a partner at the large law firm, Wachtell, Lipton, Rose & Katz, was represented by a criminal lawyer who urged on the Court his "strong belief that the goal of deterrence has already been served in this case because anyone who has followed any part of the Levine/Boesky [security fraud] cases knows what has happened to my client and knows how difficult the situation has been for him."

He then said his client was "one of those types of individuals who dedicated himself totally to the job, *billing between 2,700 and 3,300 hours a year** to achieve the status of partner."

Mr. Reich's lawyer pointed out to the listening judge that his client had now "lost his status as a superstar lawyer."

While noting that the defendant had been "a highly regarded partner in an outstanding firm at an early age" the

*All italics are the author's unless otherwise noted.

judge nevertheless said that by passing ringleader Dennis Levine illegal stolen inside information "you betrayed your trust, your family, your firm and all of us."

Judge Sweet then said:

"How did all of this come to pass? . . . As a valued associate in that firm with a potential of partnership, which was later realized, you were at the peak of your profession. You were powerful, secure, on the edge of very substantial wealth."

There was an unreal silence in the crowded courtroom on Foley Square. Then the judge summed up his message to the convicted lawyer:—

"Simply stated, a breach of trust at this level with this effect requires a jail term as a deterrent, as a statement by our society that its rules must be obeyed and that personal integrity remains a paramount requirement for our society, *particularly for those who are responsible for the enforcement and interpretation of our laws.*"

Looking down at the defendant lawyer, the judge said slowly:

"You have, it is very sad to say, become a symbol of the sickness of our society and of that loss of integrity which cannot be condoned whatever the cost."

In sentencing this law partner to jail (for the longest sentence at the time for insider trading security fraud), the judge had wondered aloud what deterrent the conviction and sentence would have on *other* lawyers by noting explicitly on the sentencing record that before the guilty plea of Ilan Reich, two other partners in Reich's law firm had been convicted of the felony of security fraud.

• Example: On June 10, 1976 Wall Street corporate lawyer Joel Dolkart—a former partner in Fried, Frank, Harris, Shriver & Jacobson and later a partner in Simpson, Thacher

& Bartlett—was convicted of forgery, based upon his plea of guilty to the 43rd count of an indictment filed against him. In essence, he was guilty of embezzlement of $2.5 million from two giant law firms. That Fall Joel Dolkart was ordered stricken from the rolls of "attorneys and counsellors-at-law" by New York's Supreme Court.

Since Joel Dolkart's conviction for fraud against his partners and his client eleven years ago, Dolkart, well acquainted in the intricacies of our Byzantine legal system, has not spent one night or day in jail.

"It's a travesty of justice," complained Justice James J. Leff, then a 57-year-old New York Supreme Court Judge, whose effort to jail Dolkart for his crimes was overturned on appeal. Subsequently Dolkart was given a sentence of 5 years' probation (no jail) on the theory he was cooperating with the New York County District Attorney and the Securities and Exchange Commission (squealing on his former corporate employer). Leniency in return for implicating former associates is perhaps customary treatment for drug dealers and other gangsters, but should it be available for members of the Bar?

"My concern," Justice Leff told a journalist at lunch one day in Little Italy, "is that the general public will now believe that the rich are treated differently than the poor, that the rich can get away with almost anything." The judge then added, plaintively:

"Lawyers are coming into my court and saying, 'why don't you treat my client the way Dolkart was treated?' And you can't blame them for asking . . . because they're right."

• Example: In the winter of 1986 a well-regarded law firm, Rogers & Wells, consented, under pressure, to pay $40 million to 330 investors who lost more than $100 million after its client J. David Dominelli's California brokerage house collapsed under the weight of fraud.

Investors charged the Rogers & Wells law firm with securities fraud, negligence and malpractice in connection with its representation of Dominelli's company. This was the largest settlement by a law firm arising out of representation of a client.

During discovery (investigation before trial) in the lawsuit, damaging evidence arose which indicated that *more than a year* before the widespread swindle surfaced some lawyers at Rogers & Wells suspected Dominelli of illegalities.

In a confidential memorandum on Rogers & Wells letterhead dated January 21, 1983, Joni Lysett Nelson, a firm partner, told of her discussions with two other partners over the activities of the client company, J. David Dominelli & Company.

The memorandum concluded that its principal, Mr. Dominelli, was probably selling unregistered securities and therefore the law firm should not represent Mr. Dominelli unless satisfied he had either registered the securities with the state or stopped selling those securities.

The Rogers & Wells firm continued to receive fees for another year until the scandal burst in the public press.

*BusinessWeek* reported that there appeared to be a reason that some partners of Rogers & Wells were reluctant to terminate its relationship with this client.

"Some six months before the Dominelli collapse, several of Rogers & Wells' most influential lawyers met to lay out their objections to dropping this lucrative client. One partner took notes. These notes provide a disquieting view of the subject being discussed by lawyers at the top of their profession that day in June 1983. The head of one section of these written notes said: '*Fees vs. Reputation.*' "

The article recalls a maxim of Yale Law School's ethics professor, Geoffrey Hazard: corporate law dedicated to "getting and keeping money" makes lawyers lose ability to be skeptical about their clients.

Rogers & Wells' presiding partner, William P. Rogers, was formerly Secretary of State and Keeper of the Seal of the United States.

• Example: James B. Stewart, a lawyer turned author, wrote *The Partners,* the story of how some large law firms have perfected the new strategy of "litigation as war." He cites the defense of IBM by Cravath, Swaine & Moore in a trial that lasted for years, developed in over 114,000 pages of trial record, lawyered by day and night legal teams.

IBM's bewildered chairman referred to the proceedings as a "Methuselah anti-trust case." It is the longest federal case in history. An IBM in-house counsel indicated that fees paid to trial counsel totaled several million dollars a year. A trial lawyer at the Cravath firm characterized the case as a "running gunfight in a sandstorm."

Stewart also chronicled the downfall of Mahlon F. Perkins, Jr., a law partner at Donovan, Leisure, Newton & Irvine, who, in the monopoly suit *Berkey Photos. v. Kodak,* perjured himself by swearing that certain subpoenaed documents had been destroyed, when in fact they had been shuttled back and forth by Perkins in suitcases to and from a rented office near the courthouse.

As a result of Perkin's false swearing, many believe that Kodak lost the trial, and Donovan Leisure lost Kodak as a client. The lawyer went to jail and a "there-but-for-the-grace-of-God" shudder went through the law profession.

• Example: The Pennzoil Company litigation against

Texaco—a giant-size battle of big oil companies and their big law firms—gives startling notice of the sheer cost of doing legal battles as if at war. Texaco, by October, 1987 had evidently spent some $55 million in legal fees on its case against Pennzoil. The trial had concluded with an $11 *billion*-dollar judgment that a jury awarded to Pennzoil in 1985 for the contested purchase by Texaco of the Getty Oil Company. This is the largest jury award in history.

After some legal shuffling, Texaco slipped into the downy protection of bankruptcy. The lawyers' legal meters continued to tick in the aftermath of the unprecedented combat. In October, Texaco's New York bankruptcy counsel asked for $2.2 million in fees and $299,000 in expenses for working over 14,300 hours from April through July. The Cravath firm—heading up Texaco's trial and appeal teams—asked for $1.5 million. Texaco must also pay for the legal expenses of the creditors' committees, estimated at $15 million a year. A shareholders' committee will cost another $7 million for bills from lawyers and their support troops of accountants, investment bankers and so-called consultants. There appeared to be no end in sight by the Fall of 1987, while one could hear the ticking of the legal meters, like a blaze of crickets, long into the night.

• Example: A number of prominent Chicago businessmen a few summers ago were invited by leaders of the local Bar to express their views of the law profession. To the consternation of the lawyers present, the business executives said they generally found lawyers overpriced, fanatical, too talkative, too combative and insufficiently concerned with the goals of their client.

• Example: Harold Kohn is a leader of the Philadelphia Bar and a first-rate trial lawyer. In a class action suit against companies alleged to have conspired to fix the price of high quality paper, Kohn found himself at odds with fellow plaintiff lawyers bringing the giant class action lawsuit.

Kohn accused his lawyer colleagues of cheating their own clients out of millions of dollars. Mr. Kohn said the issue was whether a group of attorneys should enrich themselves at the expense of their clients.

The plaintiff class action lawyers — 160 of them — fought with each other for more than 12 months over how the settlement should be split. Somehow the $50 million settlement didn't seem enough where lawyers were billing themselves out at rates as high as $650 an hour.

The bickering became public knowledge when the Federal judge on the case slashed the lawyers' fees and issued a 474-page opinion confirming Harold Kohn's courageous accusations that the lawyers in the case were more interested in lining their own pockets than in serving their 359 clients.

Harold Kohn estimated that his co-counsel had spent a combined total of *97,000 billable hours* doing a job that could just as easily have been done in 5,000 to 15,000 hours. Kohn said these lawyers let the meter run and since their fee would be "paid from the settlement fund," this meant that the lawyers were taking money that really belonged to their own clients.

* * *

By the Fall of 1987 the law firm of Finley, Kumble, Wagner, Heine, Underberg, Manley, Meyerson & Casey had grown, like Topsy, to 684 lawyers. According to Steven Brill, publisher of *The American Lawyer,* one senior partner received over $1 million a year in commissions for providing legal business to the firm without a day of practicing law at the firm.

Finley, Kumble began over twenty years ago with a group of five partners, led by Kumble. They had a vision that they could build a bigger, richer firm by being more aggressive, more "businesslike" than any firm had ever been. By 1979, they were 70 lawyers, all in New York, who had come because they would make more money there than anywhere else.

Steven Kumble was, as late as the Fall of 1987, still sanguine about the future and the ongoing success of their firm's business philosophy:

"By the early 1990's there will be a Big Eight in the legal field, just like today with accountants. The Big Eight will be on the basis of *size,* gross revenue and profitability. And Finley, Kumble will be there. Hell, we could open an office in Ames, Iowa and make it work."

A senior partner at Shearman & Sterling, Robert Caswell, sniffs at this Big Eight prototype for law firms as "not necessarily the sole and even appropriate model for Grade A firms."

At the end of 1987, the Finley, Kumble firm literally collapsed. The aggressive experiment of a megaLawFirm being "Big Business" received a jolting, traumatic setback. Finley, Kumble sank beneath the waves, its 700 lawyers scrambling desperately for another law firm life preserver. As a grim aftermath, the former Finley, Kumble partners fell to horrendous warfare over who is liable and who is responsible, court battles that may go on for years.

• Example: In April 1986, *BusinessWeek* raised the question of integrity in giant blue-chip law firms, commenting that "once unthinkable, charges of foul play are hitting prestigious [law] partnerships." One of the three items cited was in Maryland, where the savings bank industry recently was in disastrous straits. The state regulators looked for legal advice to a bright lawyer from Baltimore's Venable, Baetjer & Howard, a law firm headed by Benjamin Civiletti, a former Attorney General of the United States. According to the story, what most of the regulators did not know was that while the lawyer was advising them, his law partners were advising the same people whose questionable dealings at the edge of the law filled the regulatory agency's agenda at virtually every meeting. *BusinessWeek* commented:

"What's going on here? We're not talking about sleazy, hole-in-the-wall law firms. These are charter members of a blue-chip fraternity that has always seemed above reproach. Today, however, their names are being linked to unsavory allegations that raise serious questions about a profession whose chief asset ought to be its integrity."

In May, 1987, this large Baltimore law firm settled the State of Maryland's malpractice suit brought against it for $11 billion arising from this 1985 collapse of Maryland's savings and loan industry. The firm had engaged in a conflict of interest. A spokesman is quoted as saying that the firm doesn't believe it caused any harm; litigating the state's malpractice claim "would drain the firm's energy, resources and time," the spokesman smoothly contended.

A sensitive ethics scholar at Hofstra University Law School, Monroe H. Friedman, exclaims: "There is hubris there." The former Attorney General of the United States at the Baltimore firm, Benjamin Civiletti, candidly comments: "We should have lived up to a higher standard."

Professor Stephen Gillers of New York University Law School added darkly: "The facts about impropriety of the blue-chip Bar have been submerged and are going to start to emerge." He was prescient.

# II

# *The Character and Example of the Individual Lawyer at the Bar*

*"I am credulous about the destiny of man, and I believe more than I can ever prove of the future of the human race and the importance of illusions, the value of great expectations."*

—CARL SANDBURG

FOLLOWING ARE RECENT EXAMPLES of *individual lawyers* engaging in unacceptable behavior in their law practice, as public officials, on the bench in their role as judicial officers or in various eclectic activities as lawyers engaged in business.

In the Fall of 1982, Roy Marcus Cohn, who gained fame in the Senator Joseph McCarthy Communist Senate hearings, was charged with professional misconduct in four separate matters arising over the previous 16 years.

These charges alleged dishonesty, fraud, deceit and misrepresentation in connection with: (1) Cohn's application for admission to the Bar in Washington, D.C., (2) failure to repay a loan to a client, (3) procuring a self-serving codicil to a Will from a rich mogul who was hopelessly incompetent to execute it, and (4) violation of an escrow order of the Court by plundering the account.

For more than three years, the New York State disciplinary committee investigated with proceedings taking thousands of pages of testimony and documentary evidence.

For clarity, a word about *regulation* of the law profession.

For all its failings, the profession is deemed a "regulated industry." *Entry* into the profession and *conduct* of lawyers are subject to regulation by the highest court of each state—whether the lawyer ever goes to court or not.

Since 1970, virtually every state has in place a code of behavior based on the American Bar Association Model Code of Professional Responsibility. By 1987, over 15 states had revised their own rules to ABA Model rules adopted in 1983. The "code of ethics" that governs lawyers licensed in a particular state is the set of rules adopted by that state's highest court.

To see that the ethical codes are enforced, the courts—not the legislators—have set up disciplinary mechanisms. Some states permit the Bar associations to be of assistance in admission and enforcement of conduct standards. But the high courts have prime responsibility, and accountability; it is to these courts, as well as to legislators who revise statutes, that citizens should address reform. "Reform," says critic Anatole Broyard, "is one of the archetypal romances of American life."

On June 25, 1986, the New York Supreme Court's Appellate Division, First Department, unanimously concluded that Roy M. Cohn should be disbarred.

Since 26 years of age, bright Roy M. Cohn was always controversial and often in the storm's eye. Within a month after his disbarment he died in a hospital in Baltimore.

He will best be remembered as a relentless investigator who prosecuted the Communist spy case that sent Julius and Ethel Rosenberg to the electric chair; and as the quixotic investigator in the Senate committee hearings, where he threatened to "wreck the Army" for mistreating his friend, Gerald David Schine. With this publicity, he became thereafter a prosperous New York attorney.

Roy Cohn emerged as an example of the new fashion in success, and his ways were emulated by a growing following at the Bar. Until his death, Roy Cohn was, a large number of lawyers believed, a glamorous and intriguing leader.

Many people of repute regarded Roy M. Cohn as one of the brightest and most resilient lawyers in America. His clients included Donald Trump, the second Mrs. Henry Ford, Bianca Jagger, and former Mafia boss Carmine Galante. Cohn was gutsy. He was most articulate. He was always aggressive. He was, face it, the lawyer to hire. "People will drop a suit just by getting a letter with Roy Cohn's name at the bottom,"says Donald Trump, nodding his head.

There were some dark days. He was called before a grand jury six times. Three times he was tried and acquitted on federal charges including bribery, extortion, obstruction of justice and blackmail. He fought noisily with the Internal Revenue Service which audited him almost every year since 1959. The government claimed he owed $7 million in back taxes, interest and penalties.

To escape the tax collectors, Cohn liquidated his personal assets 25 years ago and had nothing in his name. Investigators claimed his 12-seat Merlin jet, his 96-foot yacht, his elegant Manhattan townhouse and villas in Cape Cod and Acapulco were all owned by friends of his law firm, Saxe, Bacon & Bolan. His creditors were stymied. "Just be a little smarter than they are," Cohn commented over his shoulder. Then he said archly, referring to the IRS, "that's not very difficult."

When asked what Roy M. Cohn thought of the action of the disciplinary committee against him, he replied: "They're just out to smear me up. This thing has been kicking around in hearings for three to four years. It's something

I suppose I'm going to have to learn to live with. It's not my nature to be intimidated or frightened by this bunch of yo-yo's."

Roy Cohn's law colleague, Stanley M. Friedman, who was also Bronx Democratic chairman and one of the most powerful political figures in New York City, characterized Mr. Cohn as a "fighter." (America loves a fighter.) Friedman then said, "For something this old to be still floating round against such a controversial character as Roy Cohn, I would think someone is pushing a vendetta." (America hates vendettas.) (A year or so later, Stanley M. Friedman was sentenced to 12 years in jail for public corruption and—rare in America—barred from politics for life).

Geoffrey Stokes, writing in the Village Voice, summarized William Safire's appearance as a character witness for Roy Cohn before the New York state disciplinary committee. Charles J. Hynes, a lawyer, prosecutor and a disciplinary committee member, spoke up following Mr. Safire's "good" character testimony in favor of Roy Cohn to the committee:

HYNES: "I take it you [Safire] are not aware of anything connected with the facts which are underlying the charges [against Cohn] in this case?

SAFIRE: I read the *Times* account recently, and that is all I know about. [Safire, in his column, had characterized his interrogator, committee member Hynes, as the "Torquemada" of the disciplinary committee and repeated Cohn's delicious characterization of committee members as "yo yos"].

HYNES: [modestly] Since you raise it, I would like to know the etymology because I consider myself somewhat of an etymologist.

SAFIRE: Yo-yo—like you play with . . . .Applied to individuals . . . you are working in the same area between, to use old-fashioned terminology, jerks and creeps. The jerk accenting the stupidity of the things—and the creep accenting the, perhaps, insidious nature of the attack or attacker, so that a yo-yo, in my lexicon . . . is somebody who is thoughtlessly and perhaps vindictively worthy of criticism.

HYNES: Did you think that was an accurate quote; not the interpretation, but that [it] was an accurate quote attributed to Cohn?

SAFIRE: [Always careful with words] Do I think it was an accurate quote?

HYNES: [Recovering] Do you think it was quoted accurately?

SAFIRE: Yes. And quite frankly, I think it was called for because since you are asking about this and you are asking my opinion—

HYNES: You raised it, Mr. Safire, go ahead.

SAFIRE: What is that?

HYNES: You raised it, go right ahead.

SAFIRE: [Denounces committee for "late hit," concluding:] I think it is shameful, and I think you ought to feel that shame.

HYNES: I am sorry you feel that way, but thank you for your testimony."

Stokes evenly concluded this account:

"The historical record does not reveal any witness ever having called Torquemada a jerk or a creep, but it's unlikely that the Inquisitor would have responded, 'Thank you for your testimony.' "

After 27 days of hearings in the disbarment proceedings, the state Supreme Court upheld the committee's recommendations, declaring: "For an attorney practicing law for nearly forty years in this state, such misconduct is inexcusable, notwithstanding an impressive array of character witnesses."

Toward the end of Cohn's life, when he was hospitalized and visibly ill, *New York Times* reporter, David Margolick, a legal scene observer of force, wrote a piece. Four months earlier, the disciplinary committee had recommended that Roy M. Cohn be disbarred. Mr. Margolick recognized that Mr. Cohn "has been among the most durable and distinctive figures of his generation—anathema to many, friend to the powerful, patron of politicians, confidante to cardinals." He could have added, "leader of the Bar for over two decades."

• Example: Lawyers involved in the municipal corruption in New York City by the spring of 1986 included melancholy Queens boss Donald R. Manes, who dramatically killed himself with a kitchen knife in his Queens County kitchen; Michael J. Lazar, former lawyer for Datacom Systems Corporation, a private investigator agency; and Lester N. Shafran, former director of the Parking Violations Bureau (to keep city contracts, Shafran paid bribes).

If an indicted or convicted person has a public job, appointed or elected, there is a tendency of the media to forget or ignore that the person is a *lawyer* and that the person probably practices law on the side, giving star quality to the law firm and smarmy interest to clients doing business with local and state government.

The media is apt to report that in the New York City municipal corruption tribulation that a "commissioner" was corrupt rather than, perhaps worse, that the person was a corrupt lawyer.

Or another way to view it, being a corrupt public servant *and* a corrupt lawyer is a double trust doubly broken.

• Example: On March 28, 1986 a *Times* editorial considered the Federal indictment of lawyer Stanley M. Friedman, (before his trial and conviction for fraud and bribery), mistakenly noting that by reputation he is "much too clever and well-connected an operator to resort to payoffs to win a city contract for one of his many legal clients."

Lawyer Friedman had boasted how he helped people do "business with the city" and that "No one, frankly, has got more knowledge of how government functions and operates. No one has more access to the processes in the bureaucracy than I do."

The editorial then observed that the indictment "builds an appalling picture of self-enriching influence-peddling by politicians who distracted the normally shrewd [lawyer] Mayor Koch with their vote-getting services for him." And then: "the Federal indictment portrayed audacious greed in a setting of unchallenged political power."

Nothing is said in the editorial that Stanley M. Friedman, his cohorts, Shafran and Lazar, and the Mayor himself are all licensed lawyers, who, as Judge Robert Sweet would recognize a year later, have, or should have, a special responsibility for the enforcement and interpretation of the law, not to mention the administration of justice.

In November 1986, Stanley M. Friedman was found guilty of bribery and racketeering in the New York City corruption scandal. I remember reading a story in the morning paper *after* his conviction and the reporter was making inquiry as to what Stanley M. Friedman was now doing. Lo! He was "practicing law". Friedman was then an influential partner in the law firm with which Roy M. Cohn was connected for many years. Life goes on.

Ironically, Friedman was the political boss of the Bronx where his former Bronx constituents might consider he made a fortune and where many of its people are abjectly impoverished and live in a hell called Fort Apache. Greed has its reasons which reason does not know. (I suspect that Tom Wolfe's novel, *Bonfire of the Vanities,* in its portrayal of the Bronx, was well-researched semi-fiction).

It is a sad day for Stanley M. Friedman on March 11, 1987 when he appears before Judge Whitman Knapp for sentencing. Judge Knapp distinguished himself while a lawyer as chairman of the New York City commission investigating irregularities in the New York City police department.

In the packed courtroom on Foley Square, Judge Knapp addresses lawyer Stanley M. Friedman with serious demeanor:

"You have achieved public power of the most extraordinary magnitude. Having betrayed the public trust, you should not be allowed to continue to exercise political power."

Friedman was then summarily sentenced to 12 years for conspiracy, and 5 years of probation. The second 12 years was suspended by Judge Knapp and the probation granted on the condition that "from this day forward, you will take no part, directly or indirectly, in any political activity."

Zealous prosecutor Rudolph Giuliani, drenched in the juices of righteousness, had opened the trial of Stanley M. Friedman and his colleagues in the fall of 1986—a trial that would last for eight weeks in the 100-seat Federal courtroom on-the-green in New Haven, Connecticut, with these memorable words:

"This case is about the purchase and sale of public office."

Giuliani could have added *"by lawyers."*

• Example: Federal District Court Judge Harry Claiborne of Las Vegas was convicted recently by a Federal jury of signing false income tax returns for 1979 and 1980. He failed to report $107,000. This former trial lawyer was the first Federal judge in United States history to be convicted of a crime while sitting on the bench. His appeal failed. He then challenged the right of the government to remove him on the grounds that he had been appointed by the President for life! Not unlike the boy who killed his parents and then petitioned the court for mercy because he was now an orphan. After spending 17 months in jail, wily Claiborne petitioned the Nevada Supreme Court for permission to practice law—which was granted! The court suavely ruled that consideration must be given to "the isolated nature of an attorney's conduct as well as his prior exemplary professional conduct." (In November 1987, it is revealed that lawyer-judge Claiborne had telephoned Judge Anthony M. Kennedy, then sitting on the Ninth Circuit Court of Appeals, to inquire of the status of one of Claiborne's litigated cases while a trial lawyer. Appalled at the impropriety, Judge Kennedy curtly responded: "It is under submission." Judge Kennedy has now taken a seat on the United States Supreme Court.)

* * *

• Example: On August 5, 1988, shortly before 11:00 A.M., a New York jury after a five-month trial convicted lawyer-Congressman Mario Biaggi of 15 felony counts in the Wedtech racketeering trial. Also convicted were lawyer Stanley Simon, the Former Bronx Borough President and lawyer Richard Biaggi, son of the senior member of New York City's Congressional delegation. Wedtech, a minority-oriented company, at one time a symbol of hope for the depressed inner city, became a symbol of white-collar greed and political corruption managed by lawyers.

• Example: Actress Doris Day had retained Jerome B. Rosenthal as sole attorney. She and her husband signed a written retainer agreement that gave Mr. Rosenthal a 10% interest in virtually everything they owned and earned. Rosenthal had complete control of their financial affairs until some years later when Rosenthal was terminated. He then sued Doris Day and her husband, who in turn countersued for their lawyer's breach of fiduciary duties, legal malpractice, fraud and abuse of process.

The trial court held Mr. Rosenthal liable on all counts and awarded Doris Day and her husband more than $26 million, including $1 million in punitive damages. Rosenthal appealed. The Court of Appeals affirmed the verdict against him.

On his appeal, lawyer Rosenthal argued that the verdict was invalid because no *expert* witness testified against him. The appellate court held that "expert" testimony was unnecessary to prove Rosenthal's malpractice, holding that Rosenthal "customarily thrust himself into conflicts with [Doris Day and her husband], received undisclosed profits from [their] investment, siphoned [their] money through alter ego corporations; loaned himself their money without authority and exposed [them] to losses and liabilities while avoiding personal liability himself."

The Court then lowered the boom by concluding that the

circumstances of the case "required no expert to tell the trial court [of] Rosenthal's perverted sense of duty to his clients . . ."

• Example: Watergate, 250 hours of public television, alarmed Americans with the lawlessness of lawyers. (Oddly, Irangate, where a Congressional hanging jury ironically tripped up on its own awkward questioning and the likes of Oliver North, also ran 250 hours. Perhaps that's all Americans can stand of showtime washing of our own linen).

Our hero at the Watergate hearings was the avuncular chairman, Senator Sam Ervin, an old country boy and erudite Harvard law graduate. He heard lawyer and former Attorney General of the United States John M. Mitchell insist that President Richard M. Nixon, another lawyer, knew nothing about the illegal break-in to Democratic Headquarters. (On Saturday November 12, 1988, Richard M. Nixon sat in the front pew of St. Alban's Church in Washington, D.C. at his former chief assistant's funeral. Mitchell never wrote his memoirs as most everybody else did.)

Under starry chandeliers and hot TV klieg lights, in earlier days, Senator Ervin heard at length from lawyer John Dean, twisted counsel to the President. Dean told the crowded Senate Caucus Room and a disturbed nation how President Richard M. Nixon, who had steadfastly denied all, had in fact been deeply involved in efforts to stonewall the investigation. Dean added another bombshell: Nixon kept an 'enemies' list, which titillated America by its inclusion of such adversaries as Barbara Streisand and Joe Namath, to be "screwed by available federal machinery." With this sworn testimony from a lawyer about another lawyer, Richard M. Nixon's administration and his own political career sank into ruin.

Something sour came to the public's image of lawyers' supposed service of the public interest. A dark shadow fell over the law profession. What had gone wrong?

* * *

• Example: On August 27, 1985, the highest ranking county judge in a Federal investigation of corruption in Illinois' courts, was sentenced to 2 years in prison for taking bribes and fixing traffic cases. Richard LeFevour had been convicted on 59 counts of mail fraud, racketeering and income tax violations.

He was said to have peddled justice like apples and spent money like an inebriated sailor. Prosecutors at his trial introduced evidence that a group of lawyers had paid $1,000 to $2,000 a month to Judge LeFevour so they could solicit clients.

* * *

• Example: On February 6, 1985 a practicing lawyer (until convicted of larceny), Spencer Lader, testified before a New York State Senate Committee that he participated in the bribery of several judges and other irregularities to win medical malpractice and negligence cases in New York City courts from 1979 to 1982. During the 3-year period the lawyer said he never appeared in court to handle the cases, but obtained $1.5 million in fees from law firms to which he improperly funnelled about 100 cases.

In questioning Lader, New York State Senator Jeremy Weinstein asked:

"You indicated court clerks, officers and justices were paid off. By whom? By yourself or by others?"

"By myself and others as well," Mr. Lader said.

"You said that you had proof of it by virtue of checks," Mr. Weinstein inquired, "You paid off people. You paid off justices with checks? [and then incredulously] and they *accepted* checks!?"

• Example: Aristotle used to muse that the avarice of mankind is insatiable. Ivan F. Boesky, deposed arbitrage king, comes to mind. Boesky has a law degree from Detroit Law School and for a year was law clerk to a Federal judge. He has spent a great deal of money over the years retaining and surrounding himself with lawyers. Without his circle of lawyers, prosecutors believe he could not have masterminded his schemes.

Boesky, before his plea of guilty and his sentencing to jail, was a guest of Yale's School of Organization and Management, its new business school, where he was invited to lecture on the correct manner of carrying on business. A photograph of Ivan Boesky, holding forth to the business school students, appears in the Yale business school's admissions brochure, Boesky impeccably tailored, smiling broadly.

Boesky has been quoted as to his creed, developed over his lifetime: "Greed is all right, by the way," he told a class of business students. "I think greed is healthy. You can be greedy and still feel good about yourself." According to the plea of guilty to criminal insider trading charges by investment banker Martin A. Siegel, Ivan F. Boesky literally paid in person for corporate secrets in dark downtown alleys in New York City with briefcases full of cash. Boesky was faithful to his creed of greed.

Economist John Kenneth Galbraith is asked to comment on a comparison between Ivan Boesky and the late Richard Whitney, President of the New York Stock Exchange from

1930-35, who was convicted of grand larceny in 1938 for looting New York Yacht Club stock as collateral for his own loan, among similar transgressions.

These were desperate times and Richard Whitney, a social lion and snob, needed money badly. Galbraith was asked, "Is [Boesky] the Richard Whitney of the 1980's?" Galbraith replied loftily: "He doesn't have the distinction of Richard Whitney, who was President of the [New York Stock] Exchange, a member of the Porcellian, one of the most distinguished Harvard clubs and who went into Sing Sing in a three-piece suit and with a truly aristocratic air. I don't think Mr. Boesky is quite in that league."

* * *

The United States Government has recently engaged itself in the largest crackdown in history on organized crime. The Cosa Nostra, or Mafia and its counterparts, siphon, we are told matter of factly, billions of dollars from the U.S. economy each year. Governor of New York Mario Cuomo, a smart lawyer, often struggling with nagging early-morning ethical questions, told startled reporters that there is no such thing in America as a "Mafia." After an uproar, the Governor relented somewhat. He may still be undecided about that. This incident is said to have haunted his announced decision not to run for President of the United States in 1988.

Armed with powerful laws and wider use of electronic eavesdropping, the Federal government has obtained over 4,000 organized crime indictments in the last few years alone. (Some prosecutors have even begun in 1987 bringing *civil* actions against alleged Mafia families, an annoyance professional criminals find unbearable). The heads of 16 of the nation's 24 Mafia families have been indicted in the last five years. To the eager prosecutors' chagrin, they were unsuccessful in snaring alleged Mafia chieftain John Gotti who, after acquittal by the jury in Brooklyn Federal court, in mid-March 1987, "took a walk" in one of his handsome $2,000 suits. Nobody is perfect, and some indicted people are innocent. (In January 1989, Gotti was indicted again for attempted murder of a union official). It is the law of the land, steadily ignored by the populace, that an accused person is presumed innocent until convicted by a court or a plea of guilty.

Today professional criminals are becoming sophisticated. The third generation now turns to lawyers to protect their vested empire of drug trafficking, labor racketeering and gambling.

Judge Irving R. Kaufman of the United States Court of Appeals for the Second Circuit was tapped by President Reagan as chairman of the Commission on Organized Crime. Chairman Kaufman, who continued on the bench as a jurist, finds a "disturbing trend" in the flow of lawyers serving the interests of organized crime groups.

Some law enforcement officers believe that these lawyers may be as suspect as the mobsters. In March 1985, a staff study of the Commission charged that a small group of "renegade attorneys" helps supply the "life-support system of organized crime." The report stated that these lawyers have become "integral parts" of today's complex criminal enterprises.

Lawyers direct the laundering of illicit money through myriad banks, restaurants, real estate investments and other transactions. (Laundering money, properly understood, means *paying* taxes on illicit cash to legitimize it.) Lawyers give legal advice to cut down on arrests and convictions. They employ the attorney-client confidentiality privilege to shield the mobsters, even making available their own law offices as places for development of new schemes under an attorney's shield of confidentiality.

Judge Kaufman, a skilled Federal prosecutor before going on the bench at an early age, says that when lawyers commit crimes to "protect the leaders of criminal cartels" the result is not only a "*crisis of confidence in the bar,* but a law enforcement problem of serious magnitude."

The Kaufman Commission staff members estimate that the professional crime Bar consists of about 200 lawyers coast to coast, mostly in Miami, New York, Chicago and Las Vegas. Judge Kaufman is concerned that unethical lawyers are part of a general threat within the profession. He warns:

"Unquestioning advancement of a client's wishes at all costs is a destructive notion that undermines the foundation of the [law] profession."

The Mafia's businesses, in order, are restaurants, nightclubs, garbage collection, trucking, air freight, fast-food outlets, banks, travel agencies, construction, and pornography. Two insights: (1) you can tell which areas are involved just by observing where *delays* are costly and (2) organized crime needs those places where money illicitly obtained can be laundered.

The International Association for the Study of Organized Crime for the President's Commission on Organized Crime, lists Mafia crimes, in order, as murder, extortion, racketeering, labor racketeering, loansharking, gambling, prostitution, drugs, bribery of public officials, highjacking, burglary and credit card fraud.

* * *

Despite these transgressions illustrated in this chapter, most lawyers will blandly say that the practice of law has not changed much and that the attitudes and outlook are the same today as years ago, dusting off early day chicanery such as Teapot Dome and Sir Francis Bacon's bribe-taking in old London while serving on the bench. The majority of attorneys also will insist that there has been no increase in wrongdoing, malpractice and self-dealing by lawyers in the past twelve years.

Statistics indicate, to the contrary, that in the past decade, wrongdoing, conflicts, breaches of legal ethics and malpractice have in fact risen significantly, leading to debate only as to what extent. Abuses have become more *brazen* as well. There is always another well-paid lawyer out there to defend, for dollars, the fellow lawyer accused of breach of ethics and violations of the law. Everyone does it, they say.

Professor Stephen Gillers sees a "stunning" increase in actions *against* lawyers in the last ten years. "Lawyers," he says, "once untouchable, are now among the most *vulnerable of all professions.*"

Between 1984 and 1985 (most recent figures), complaints against lawyers rose 35%. An Ohio law professor, William L. Tabac, states that malpractice cases against lawyers have risen sharply in the past twelve years.

These studies indicate that many charges of malpractice against lawyers are settled immediately, to avoid publicity, loss of license and, of course, ruined reputation. Often these cases go unrecorded for statistical purposes.

The truth is that the statutory power of disciplinary committees and the higher courts to disbar a lawyer for misconduct is rarely invoked. Roy M. Cohn is one exception.

There is an illogical tacit understanding in the justice system that if a lawyer is once blessed with a license to practice, it will not be revoked. This is—in view of current endemic misbehavior — a serious error of perception. A lawyer disbarred is not dropped off the cliff, but is free to engage in an enormous scope of activity — *outside* the profession. He has not the right to demand, despite his breaches of conduct, that he remain, as if a vested right to further perfidy has set in, like rigor mortis.

One difficulty, ironically, is that disciplinary committees are timid and hesitant to disbar because the committee members can be, and often are, sued by the disbarred lawyer! The same difficulty is apparent in the medical profession. State medical licensing boards rarely de-license a physician no matter how grievous his conduct may be as an alcoholic, drug addict, criminal, senile person or just plain incompetent. In 1985 (last figures available), only 2,108 of the 550,000 physicians in the United States — less than four-tenths of one per cent — were even *subject* to serious disciplinary proceedings by the state medical boards.

Experts say the reason is the same for lawyers' disciplinary committees: they are afraid of being sued: the personal expense, the time, the aggravation! But the wiser medical profession moved swiftly to relieve this impairment of the medical system by introducing a new Federal law, which provides that the suing doctor can be compelled to pay the medical board's litigation expenses if the board is found to have acted in good faith. This intelligent protection is extended to state and local medical societies.

The same protection should be extended to the state disciplinary committees overseeing the conduct of lawyers. From such reform the fabric of the Bar will be strengthened and uplifted to the benefit of the public at large. No reason to remain in a quagmire.

* * *

Received wisdom indicates only one out of about 12 lawsuits actually ever gets to trial. Why then the large litigation expense? Discovery, that endless pretrial process that drives most people up the wall. Charles Elias Clark, former Dean of Yale Law School (later a well-regarded judge on the Federal Second Circuit Court of Appeals), drafted new Federal Civil Procedure rules in the 1930's with the thought that *full discovery* prior to trial would lead to *shorter* and *less expensive* litigation, all in the interest of justice.

Everyone was elated. Dawn of a new era. But today lawyer abuses and overkill have made the discovery process in the United States cost as much as 80% of the bill in commercial litigation.

Young lawyers love discovery. They are weaned on it. At cocktail parties they say they are litigators (read gladiators). Laura Saunders of *Forbes* laid out an insightful laymen's guide to abusive litigation discovery:

"Ask lawyers if they use discovery as a tactic to delay, confound or financially drain their opponents, and they are aghast at such a notion. It is remarkable, though, how often their unscrupulous colleagues had tried to do it to them." She concludes: "One wonders what ever happened to [Judge Charles E. Clark's] first rule of the civil procedure, which says that the purpose of the rules is to 'secure the just, speedy and inexpensive outcome of an action.' "

* * *

While serving as Chief Justice of the United States Supreme Court, Warren E. Burger took the lead, against a strong tide, to prod the American Bar to higher standards of public service and ethical practices, including more skillful, less costly, performance in our over-stuffed trial courts.

Chief Justice Burger took his case annually to the American Bar Association convention. This is the largest and most influential Bar association, to the extent that a giant association can affect the quality and behavior of lawyers in general, half of whom do not choose to be members.

Chief Justice Burger, gifted with golden arrows of oratory, took aim at one of the modern abuses of lawyers:

"The American legal profession — lawyers, judges, law teachers—has become so mesmerized with the stimulation of the courtroom context that we tend to forget that we ought to be *healers* of conflicts. Doctors, in spite of astronomical medical costs, still retain a high degree of public confidence because they are perceived as healers. Should lawyers not be healers? Healers, not warriors? Healers, not procurers? Healers, not hired guns?"

Lawyer response to the Chief Justice's admonition was mixed. Judges and law teachers were largely silent. For the most part, lawyers themselves were feeding and did not like being disturbed.

Chief Justice Burger did, however, get a favorable response from lawyer Harvey J. Kaufman, who, on Valentine's Day, wrote the *New York Times:*

"As an attorney in practice for over 20 years, I generally disagree vehemently with Chief Justice Burger's comment concerning lawyers. However, I have to regard the Chief Justice's description of a segment of the Bar as 'procurers' as being particularly appropriate when the response of the lawyers to whom this appellation is addressed is to accord the speaker a standing ovation."

Thereafter, the indefatigable Chief Justice goaded the American Bar Association hierarchy, including some of its venerable former presidents, to set up a Commission to inquire into the standards currently maintained by the American law profession and to make recommendations. (A commission is made up of laymen as well as lawyer members).

Although the Commission had eminent members and an able chairman, Justin A. Stanley, a former president of the American Bar Association, and a good staff, (Richard Solomon was the secretary of the Commission), its report was considered by many reformers as opaque and hesitant, and has been generally ignored.

In a final address to the American Bar Association as America's Chief Justice, Warren Burger offered a review of his principal themes — opposition to advertising by lawyers, concern about the contingency fee system, and unhappiness at the behavior of some U.S. lawyers after the Bhopal gas disaster.

"What people think of the legal profession — the bench and the bar — is very important to us and it is important to the country.

"During the last dozen years or so, many of us have had growing concern whether our profession was turning away from traditional values and standards and becoming more and more like a common trade in the marketplace."

* * *

• Example: On Tuesday, February 17, 1987, a 34-year-old New York lawyer, Israel G. Grossman, was led, in handcuffs, from his law firm's office at 10:45 a.m. by four government agents. He was arrested on criminal charges of stealing inside information from his law firm. He illegally misused information about a pending recapitalization at Colt Industries, a firm client.

Immediately after learning that information, Mr. Grossman made more than forty telephone calls to relatives and friends in a 6-day period. Most bought stock options of

Colt, whose stock soared after Colt made public its plan to repurchase its stock. The profits to Mr. Grossman and his tipped associates amounted to over $1.4 million.

On August 18, 1987 a New York Federal jury convicted Grossman of insider-trading charges after a two-week trial on Foley Square. This was to be the first criminal case of this kind in two years that the government had to prove in court. Other indicted lawyers and non-lawyers had chosen to plead guilty before trial in the desperate hope for a lesser sentence—at all cost to avoid being remanded to jail. After three hours of jury deliberation, the 34-year-old Grossman was convicted of all 38 counts of securities fraud and mail fraud.

Then, to observers' surprise, Grossman was immediately ordered jailed after prosecutors said there was a risk that if bailed, pending his sentencing and appeal, this lawyer would flee the country.

On September 15, 1987, Grossman was sentenced to two years in jail and fined $25,000 by Judge Richard Owen. Grossman, with relatives and friends, had invested $33,937.54 and made profits in a few days totalling $1,467,344.57.

# PART TWO

## *III. What Happened to the American Law Profession?*

## *IV. Legal Narcissism, Manners and Morals*

*"Highmindedness, magnanimity, courtesy, justice and generosity are much more in accordance with nature than pleasure, richness or even life itself."*

—MARCUS TULLIUS CICERO
Member of the Roman Bar, 58 B.C.

# III

## *What Happened to the American Law Profession?*

*"The measure of a civilization is the degree of its obedience to the unenforceable."*

—LORD MOULTON

FOR TWO CENTURIES American lawyers have provided leadership in government, institutions, business and public opinion—as well as providing objective advice to private clients.

The founders of our republic were lawyers. Lawyers served to preserve our liberty. Our fundamental documents—the Declaration of Independence, the Constitution and the Bill of Rights—are primarily the work of lawyers. What has happened?

In addition to the sordid examples and the comments of critics set forth above, there persists other cumulative evidence showing grave decline in American lawyers' professionalism. Worse, the decline has grown dramatically in the last 12 years.

Upholding basic traditional principles of the law profession is not really an onerous, hair-shirted burden to be avoided at all costs by red-blooded adventurers. The rules are natural and functional, not precious or artificial. There is no call here for angels at the Bar. Man's laws are imperfect but nonetheless it is the first task of the lawyer to uphold the laws. The drama, "A Man for All Seasons" has a scene portraying the martyrdom of Sir Thomas More, Lord Chancellor of England, for turning down Henry VIII's declaration of the supremacy of the Crown over the Church. In dialogue with his son-in-law, William Roper, Sir Thomas More speaks:

"The law, Roper, the law. I know what's legal, not what's right. And I'll stick to what's legal."

Roper replies: "So now you'd give the Devil the benefit of the law!"

Sir Thomas More: "Yes. What would you do? Cut a great road through the law to get after the Devil?"

Roper: "I'd cut down every law in England to do that!"

Sir Thomas More: "Oh? And when the last law was down and the Devil turned round on you, where would you hide, Roper, *the laws all being flat?*"

* * *

Another cause of decline in the profession, besides warped attitude and short-sighted outlook — largely unknown to the public—is severe, economic pressures growing wildly on lawyers and law firms, large and small, throughout the country. Enormous expenses (rents, salaries, malpractice insurance, promotion, ruinous purchase prices for acquiring lawyer rainmakers from Congress or other firms) are cutting down profits, wilting the coveted draw of the partners. We are beginning to see the harrowing results of these current economic inroads. That bigness does not always lead to success—or even big profits—is the hard lesson being learned.

Dean Roscoe Pound's definition of the law profession as "the practice of a learned art in the public interest" seems anachronistic in today's world whether in Boston or Los Angeles or in between.

(Webster's New International Dictionary defines a "profession" as both a calling and a claim. The three professions—often referred to as the *learned* professions—are acknowledged as a name for the professions of (1) *theology,* (2) *law,* and (3) *medicine.* Members are obligated to conform to technical and ethical standards of the profession. A profession then is "a calling in which one professes to have acquired some special knowledge used by way either of instructing, guiding or advising others or servicing them in some art".)

To show how far nowadays members of our society have stretched the meaning of "professional," there is the recent illustration in New York City of a homeless person (Miss Joyce Brown) defying Mayor Koch's edict that she must be confined to an institution. Miss Brown at the hearing confidently argued that she was a "professional" street person, capable of surviving, noting that she planned to return to a hot air vent at Second Avenue near 65th Street where she lived.

In 1920, R. H. Tawney, a Fellow of Balliol College, Oxford, wrote *The Acquisitive Society,* arguing that *all business* should be converted to professionalism on the theory that such transformation would upgrade the morals and standards of business. Industry must, he insisted, become a profession. Professor Tawney believed that all social institutions are the visible expression of the scale of moral values which rules the minds of individuals, and it is "impossible to alter institutions without altering that moral valuation." His novel and perceptive concept was intellectually entertained but got nowhere.

A brilliant lawyer and judge took another tack. He asked: Can the law profession be more finely defined? Benjamin N. Cardozo understood the essential nature and function of the law profession early on. He pointed out that a lawyer is not a "journeyman" devoted to his own interests but has a duty to his profession arising out of its special nature: the lawyer's exclusive franchise to practice law and his or her vital role in the administration of justice.

This is why ordinary—otherwise acceptable—marketplace behavior is destructive *inside* the legal profession.

Justice Cardozo was the first to recognize fully the extent to which all members of the Bar are, or should be, "officers of the court," not as juniors, subservient to the sitting judges, but rather as responsible participants in the overall administration of our *justice system.* Justice Cardozo discovered, through his meticulous research, that this concept arose in England where the solicitor (office lawyer), and even the barrister (court lawyer), are historically obligated to be an "instrument to enhance justice" and therefore owe a special responsibility of *care* for the justice system.

This inherited concept is more significant than it seems, because in any civilization, the state of the justice system is the bedrock of the quality of life. Breakdown of America's justice system is the single most haunting specter today. If justice goes, all goes.

A lawyer, recognizing this inherent duty, is professional only while independent, free to perform professional obligations objectively — to clients, to the courts and to the public interest. Above all, true professionalism rises above self-interest.

Albert Einstein told us that the problems of the world are not induced by sinners but rather "by those who passively sit by and let it happen." Edmund Burke, the Anglo-Irish advocate, once exclaimed to Parliament that all that is necessary for the triumph of evil is that good men do nothing.

The downward fall of the law profession has the insidious

effect of not only bringing crisis to the American Bar but also to American *life* because the lawyer in the United States is such an *integral* part of all activity.

Lawyers are community leaders (good or bad) and run our government on all levels. The late Mr. Justice Robert H. Jackson once wrote, while on the United States Supreme Court, that in America the "administration of justice is based on *law practice.*" (italics his).

Go anywhere. Listen anywhere. Too many of the 800,000 lawyers in the United States show signs of having lost their way. "When a nation goes down, or a society perishes," Carl Sandburg reminded us, "one condition may always be found: they forgot where they came from." Who ever stops to consider the ancient—and noble—origins and purpose of the law practice we inherited from England? We simply assume in a modern world we can do our own thing without any old-fashioned need to glance backward for insights for the future.

That prescient observer of early America, Alexis de Tocqueville, declared in *Democracy in America:*

"If you ask me where the American aristocracy is found, I have no hesitation in answering that it is not among the rich who have no common link uniting them. It is at the bar or the bench that the American aristocracy is found."

At that time it was, for the most part, an aristocracy of ability, quality and independence.

The way lawyers present themselves to the public is a curious barometer of the extent the profession adheres to basic standards of performance. Advertising and marketing reveal the goals of the lawyers which in turn determine their behavior patterns.

There is the unseemly competition for "business" bringing rising aggressiveness and incivility. Lawyers have been told by the United States Supreme Court in 1977 that they have a constitutional *right* to advertise. To have a right doesn't mean that it must be exercised, or exercised in bad taste, or with innuendo of misleading promise. Do you want a divorce cheap? Have you considered welshing on your debts by inexpensive bankruptcy? If you were in an automobile accident, are you sure you don't have whiplash or a permanent back injury? The legal as well as the psychological impact of the Supreme Court decision has been enormous.

* * *

Other changes in the law practice are as dramatic. Twelve years ago, there were few law firms which had as many as a hundred lawyers. Today, three-hundred-lawyer firms, at least in large cities, are considered medium-sized firms. Today, we have megaLawFirms, firms of 600, 800, over 1000 lawyers.

Twelve years ago, it was virtually unheard of for a partner in a major law firm to leave that law firm for "opportunity" in another law firm, often taking a passel of clients with him. Today, lawyers are moving around like whirling dervishes.

Twelve years ago, it was unheard of for lawyers to raid other law firms to get partners who have the desired clients attached to their watch fobs. Law firms are now openly raiding clients and lawyers from other law firms—and they are proud of it.

There is now one paid consultant firm to law firms, which advises firms to put together what is called a "hit list" of clients that the firms would *like* to have who would "fit in" with their practice. The hit list is euphemistically called "new professional opportunities," and these consultants tell you that if you cannot steal the client, then steal the lawyer who controls the client.

Twelve years ago, more firms were managed by an old-timer lawyer, and management consisted of being certain that everyone had enough pencils and legal pads. Today, firms are run by professional manager-accountants, the new barbarians, who are not lawyers, have, with some exception, no real knowledge of the profession, and who sometimes have more power than senior partners.

The quiet revolution is here, and the revolt raises several questions. First, what do lawyers do about it? Do they merge to try to get bigger? Do they contract to form boutique law firms specializing in such esoterics as environmental law, age discrimination or energy law? Or do they peel off like World War I ace pilots to practice law with four to six lawyers, using outside counsel as needed?

Is what is happening enhancing the profession and society? Or, are we creating a breed of monopolizing lawyers with no sense of history and narrow education, riveted to their own self-interest?

Today the pace quickens, as we are driven along in a period of exponential spectacular change: notable for its swarms of paralegals, advertising and PR, rudeness and crudeness, clogged courts, armies of lawyers. We become a more litigious society; innovative claims abound; hardball competition among lawyers is rampant. As the profession becomes a business, there follows, as night the day, a marked decline in public confidence in the American Bar. Lawyers stand—or lie—at the bottom of the barrel.

* * *

A Yale Law Professor and public servant, Eugene V. Rostow, addressed law students at a traditional ritual—the law journal banquet. He asked them Supreme Court Justice Oliver Wendell Holmes' *classic* question about law:

"How can the laborious study of a dry and technical system, the greedy watch for clients and practice of the shopkeeper's arts, the mannerless conflicts over often sordid interests, make out a life?"

Holmes' answer to this Delphic question, with which Professor Rostow agreed, was that "if a man has a soul of Sancho Panza, the world to him will be Sancho Panza's world, but if he has the soul of an idealist, he will make—I do not say find—his world ideal."

"The work of a lawyer," Holmes said elsewhere, "is work for thinkers . . . and what distinguishes great lawyers from journeymen is the *quality* of their thought."

The root of the problem is that too many lawyers have forgotten the *purpose* of the law profession — to serve the public interest. As the late Supreme Court Justice Potter Stewart declared, " . . . the practice of law is a *profession*. It is not like making shoes or making autombiles."

* * *

The shoot-em-up way the American Bar litigates today is unheard of in other countries; unheard of 25 years ago in this country. Abraham Lincoln advised the younger generation of lawyers to discourage litigation. "Persuade your neighbors to compromise whenever you can. Point out to them how the nominal winner is often a real loser—in fees, expenses, and waste of time. As a peacemaker the lawyer has a superior opportunity of being a good man." Times have changed.

The peculiar nature of the law profession is of essentially intimate quality which cannot, without changing professional substance, be mass-produced on assembly lines while accountants watch, with number 2 pencils, for inefficiencies on the computer screens.

Mr. Justice Lewis F. Powell, Jr. wrote recently that Justice Potter Stewart was the closest friend on the Court of the late Justice John Marshall Harlan—an exceptional lawyer and judge. Justice Stewart was given the sad duty of delivering Harlan's letter of retirement to the President. After Harlan's death, Justice Stewart wrote: "[W]hat truly set [Justice Harlan] apart was his *character* . . . his generous and gallant spirit, his selfless courage . . . his total decency."

Joseph W. Bartlett, a former law clerk to the late Chief Justice Earl Warren (and now a successful metropolitan lawyer) writes an open letter (published in *American Heritage*) about fundamental changes in the practice of law since his United States Supreme Court clerkship. (His old boss by now has gone to his reward.)

"Also, I anticipated that lawyers would enjoy great prestige in the community. On this point I was largely wrong. Individual lawyers may still be highly regarded, but *as a class they are more typically reviled* . . . unfortunately, it's not easy these days to be an ethical lawyer. . . . I now have close to one-hundred partners, about ten times as many as when I first joined what was then a family firm. . . . I am a specialist — I have to be to survive. The days of the general practitioner, in urban areas, anyway, are numbered . . . lawyers are no longer as magisterial as they once were. We advertise openly for business, we hustle clients. . . . On the other hand, the profession is more open . . . [overall] I find the profession's atmosphere of relentless selfishness is depressing for me as a citizen to be sure, but it is particularly saddening to me as a lawyer.

"We need a rejuvenation [Bartlett continues], a force to

turn our heads away from the giant amounts of money some of us are making toward the responsibilities that a ticket to practice law used to impose. We are parts of big organizations now, but most of us, deep down, are still sole practitioners.

"Maybe that spirit can be revived—the independent attorney-at-law, to whom you turn if you are in trouble. I hope so."

# IV

## *Legal Narcissism, Manners and Morals*

*The bad drives out the good.*

*Gresham's Law.*

ALL AMERICA SUFFERS an epidemic of rudeness and crudeness, observes Miss Manners (aka Judith Martin) in her broadside *Common Courtesy,* in defense of civility.

How, Miss Manners asks, can we keep our uncivil professional lives from destroying our private lives? She insists that manners are not an affectation of the wealthy to annoy the poor, but rather codes of conduct used by people of all classes.

"The most sophisticated and ruthless enforcers of manners with rigid regulations about dress, speech and hierarchy are teen-aged street gangs," Miss Manners points out—didactically.

From my own observation of these street gangs, I conclude that manners, or outward codes of surface behavior, have little to do with morals. Well-mannered persons can be outrageous criminals.

For example, Frank Costello, who was convicted of Federal tax evasion, always wore a grey hat, yet charmed us all as the top man of the mob; the Mafia's number one, Albert Anastasia, who was blasted to death while being shaved, luxuriously, in the Park Sheraton Hotel near Central Park; Aaron Burr, whom women adored before and after he killed Alexander Hamilton; Hollywood's own George Raft, portraying the suave racketeer with five o'clock shadow; Willie Sutton, who disarmed the man who asked why he robbed banks, with, "Because that's where the money is"; Clarence Darrow, great artist of cross-examination, twice criminally charged with suborning perjury, and twice acquitted after long trials; gentleman clubman Richard Whitney, who, during the depression's stress, robbed everyone blind including his children's trusts. And who is smoother or more charming than Alger Hiss? Gentlemanly all.

But while all well-mannered folks are not necessarily moral, all moral folks are generally well-mannered.

Assuming that is true, what about the manners and morals of the legal profession today, particularly its 80,000 litigators, the sometimes flamboyant egocentric trial Bar? Have many descended to low standards of behavior? None admits he or she has.

The Supreme Court of the United States recently took time to issue its own ukase on manners and behavior in our American court system:

Our highest court decreed that a lawyer's "single incident of rudeness or lack of professional courtesy" does not render him unfit for practice. See *Robert J. Snyder, Petitioner,* 472 U.S. 105 (1985).

From the plains of North Dakota, a young trial lawyer named Snyder had the nerve to criticize the way the former Chief Judge of the Eighth Circuit handled his lawyer fee claim for his assignment to represent a defendant under the Criminal Justice Act. In his letter to the trial court, he complained about the "extreme gymnastics [necessary] even to receive the puny amounts."

His application had been returned because it was "insufficiently documented." The lawyer, enraged, said he could provide no more because his computer software had technical problems and he told the court he was not "sending you anything else." Then the final blow to the Federal court: "You can take it or leave it."

The Eighth Circuit's Chief Judge considered Snyder's letter "*totally disrespectful* to the Federal courts and to the judicial system." After Snyder refused to apologize, the Chief Judge wrote him a scarlet letter, angrily noting Mr. Snyder's "disrespect," then admonishing him: "*You serve as an officer of the court* and, as such, the Canons of Ethics require every lawyer to maintain a respect for the court as an institution."

Again, Snyder refused to apologize for what he termed "telling the truth, albeit in harsh terms." That did it! He was suspended from practice in the Eighth Circuit.

Former Chief Justice Warren Burger wrote the mannerly opinion for the United States Supreme Court, reversing the judgement below. He held, "even assuming that [Snyder's] letter exhibited an unlawyer-like rudeness, a single incident of rudeness or lack of professional courtesy—in this context—does not support a finding of contemptuous or contumacious conduct or a finding that a lawyer is 'not presently fit to practice in the Federal courts.' Nor does it rise to the level of 'conduct unbecoming a member of the bar' warranting suspension from practice."

In dissecting the issue of lawyers' manners, the Supreme Court recognized that members of the Bar are subject to a "complex code of behavior" wherein they have a dual obligation to clients *and* to the "system of justice."

The Court then quoted Justice Benjamin N. Cardozo, whose ringing words have done much to uphold the fading professionalism of the American Bar:

" 'Membership in the bar is a privilege *burdened with conditions.*' [An attorney is] received into that ancient fellowship for something more than private gain. He [becomes] an *officer of the court, and, like the court itself, an instrument or agency to advance the ends of justice.*"

Chief Justice Burger than magnanimously broadened the requirements of courtesy in the courts to encompass *everyone.* "All persons involved in the judicial process—judges, litigants, witnesses and court officers—owe a duty of courtesy to all other participants." There you have it.

Narcissism breeds incivility and vice. Behavioral scientists derive this label from Greek mythology's young Narcissus gazing pleasurably at his own reflected self. A narcissistic person is essentially stunted in emotional growth: he wants it when he wants it and he wants it *now.*

For short, he is a "narce." Our society may have more narces today than at any other time in history. In the last decade narces have evidently captured control of many large law firms where they have infused narrow notions of preoccupation with self, eschewing concern for others and long-range vision. They substitute adrenaline for judgment.

There are a number of reasons to believe that narces are more common in the megaLawFirms than in smaller ones. Simply put, narces survive well in a big firm because their *attitudes* and *perspectives* fit better into a pattern where the good is the computerized bottom line, rather than service of community interest.

The shortcomings of the narce are less evident in a multi-leveled bureaucratic environment. The megaLawFirms rely heavily on the computer rather than on personal relations.

Elements of altruism, loyalty, collegiality, grace, judgment, integrity or just common decency cannot be registered or printed out on a computer. This recent discovery is the everlasting joy of the narce.

The narce says, "look at the billable hours I have dictated." "Look at my *winnings.*" "Look at my revenues I have brought in this quarter." "Look at my clients on *my* list," taking an envelope out of his pocket.

The narces, because of these factors, have a better chance for promotion to partner in the big firm and even to the firm's management committee.

Because the law profession in the United States is an essential part of the administration of justice, the introduction of narcissism is particularly harmful. Narces invade the profession because there is no screen except grades. Character and mental health are totally irrelevant if not embarrassingly improper to even discuss.

* * *

An astonishing revelation (I found by accident) relates to lawyers' inherent narcissism, manners and morals in a most unexpected place. In Chapter XVII (in the years A.D. 300 – 500) is Edward Gibbon's lively account of the rise of a misbehaving lawyer body infesting the Roman law profession with bad manners and morals. The event and timing is revealing.

The curious source is *The Decline and Fall of the Roman Empire.* By this time the Roman Empire had been insensibly in decline for several hundred years. Lawyer services had been provided by an educated, public-service minded small group, exclusively licensed to give true counsel to the individual and the state.

Soon, however, Gibbon reports, this "lucrative science" was invaded by a large number of youthful materialists hot for riches and a generous share of the government of the republic.

Law schools sprang up throughout the Empire in cities East and West. The most famous, or infamous, was in Beirut, on the coast of Phoenicia; it flourished for 300 years.

After a five-year course, these Roman law students went out in search of their fortune. Gibbon mischievously notes that there was an "inexhaustible supply of business [for the new lawyers] in a great empire already corrupted by the multiplicity of laws, of arts, and of vices."

Gibbon graphically describes how the new swarm of lawyers behaved, or misbehaved, as new members of the Roman Empire Bar, revealing their novel concepts of punctilio of honor and their blindness to inherent obligations of their newly-acquired law profession:

"In the practice of the Bar, these men had considered reason as the instrument of dispute; they interpreted the laws according to the dictates of private interest, and the same pernicious habits might still adhere to their characters in the public administration of the state.

"The honour of a liberal profession has indeed been vindicated by ancient and modern advocates, who have filled the most important stations with pure integrity and consummate wisdom; but in the decline of Roman jurisprudence the ordinary promotion of lawyers was pregnant with mischief and disgrace. . . .

"Some of them procured admittance into families for the purpose of fomenting differences, of encouraging suits, and of preparing a harvest of gain for themselves or their brethren.

"Others, recluse in their chambers, maintained the gravity of legal professors by furnishing a rich client with subtleties to confound the plainest truth and with arguments to colour the most unjustifiable pretensions.

"Careless of fame and of justice, they are described for the most part as ignorant and rapacious guides who conducted their clients through a maze of expense, of delay, and of disappointment, from whence, after a tedious series of years, they are at length dismissed when their patience and fortune were almost exhausted."

Gibbon's history gives a detailed tapestry of the decline of the dedicated Roman law profession, in another age, over 1500 years ago.

Those who choose to ignore history, Santayana suggested, are condemned to have it repeated.

# PART THREE

## *V Rise of the MegaLawFirm*

## *VI Morals of the Marketplace*

## *VII Lawyers as Thick as Locusts*

*"The life of the law has not been logic; it has been experience."*

—OLIVER WENDELL HOLMES, JR.
Introduction, *The Common Law*

# V

## *Rise of the MegaLawFirm*

*"Business is Booming"* — Refrain.

AS AMERICAN SOCIAL, economic and political structures evolve and change, so must its institutions and so must the practice of law. This is a given. Kiekegaard taught correctly that "life can only be understood backwards, but must be *lived* forwards."

What is significant is whether the *fundamental* changes taking place in the professional practice of law are necessary or desirable. We must be careful to discern whether the inevitable change is to make things bigger and bigger, or to make the quality of service and the quality of life better and better.

The principal change in the last twelve years in the legal profession has been the transformation of the legal profession into a business enterprise. Never before has this basic shift been as openly touted and openly performed. The giant law firms have become like business corporations in their structure, management and goals.

In the last year, between 1988 and 1989, America has witnessed emergence of the so-called "law industry" as the number one business service provided in our economy. During 1988 alone, 100 American law firms grossed over $10.5 *billion,* according to the most recent *The American Lawyer* survey (August, 1989).

* * *

A firm of high reputation, White & Case, seemed to critics in recent years to run aground on the notion, widely bandied about, that it wasn't "aggressive" enough, was "too gentlemanly" and rewarded partners on the basis of seniority and experience. This firm did not follow the fashion at this time that you only eat what you kill. It had followed, rather, Rene Dubos' dictum that *destiny need not follow trend.* As long as I can remember, White & Case was a fine legal and ethical law firm. This was the general view.

Pressures mounted, however, spurred perhaps by younger partners, (and the thought that if a law practice had continued for many years it is ripe for "efficiency") resulting in the appointment, and reappointment, of a czar to handle management — business-getter (rainmaker), James Hurlock. He took the helm, it is reported, with zealous determination. Many of his partners laud his insistent emphasis on *accountability* determined by the almighty computer.

Partner Raynor Hamilton, who served for several years on the management committee, offered, this telling comment about the volatile James Hurlock:

"He has changed the firm from a men's club environment to a *business* by emphasizing that *each of us is a profit center.*"

A precipitous change of this character may bring with it deep troubles to the Bar as a whole. Becoming an efficient machine and urging every partner to be "a profit center" has its own special consequences on *how* the partners behave, *how* they go about counseling clients and *how* they serve community interests. It is not the salient purpose of the law profession to focus so specially, so exclusively on *profits* and on *efficiency* (the same concept, euphemistically). Indeed, to do so is directly counter to the essence of what the profession is about.

This is not to say that it is evil to make money. What is wrong is that the law profession by reason of its nature and function is not an appropriate vehicle for exalting profits over other values. If a lawyer wants to exalt profits he can, and many do, leave the profession for other lines of acquisitive endeavor such as leveraged buyouts, fueled by junk bonds. No one has a constitutional right to practice law on one's own terms.

While there have always been some lawyers and law firms who, covertly or not, operated as a trade and ignored professional standards, the *immense* shift to the business ethos of growing giant firms has been extraordinary—and harmful to society.

These giant firms comprise, unbelievably, only about four or five per cent of the Bar. Yet their enormous *power* and *example* make this revolution stunning, leading to undermining consequences to the bedrock purpose of the legal profession.

Many megaLawFirm leaders chose to excuse their law firms. Over forty-seven *billion* dollars in legal fees is paid annually to lawyers. Despite such huge sums, lawyer and non-lawyer managers of the large law firms insist that competitive pressures are "forcing" lawyers to abandon traditional goals and obligations and to become tradesmen in a vast lucrative marketplace. The pretense is slyly offered that rapid economic forces shape the law profession into a trade, *not* the choice of the law firm's management. They *had* to do it to survive. Put another way, they had to abandon professionalism to provide themselves with profits for high and powerful living. Necessity is the plea for every infringement of professional standards. As William Pitt the Younger said in his speech to the House of Commons in 1783, "It is the argument of tyrants; it is the creed of slaves."

The continued surge of the megaLawFirms is a stunning phenomenon—all within current memory and experience. In 1948 when I clerked at Root, Ballantine, Harlan, Bushby & Palmer, three lawyers who had not made partner, left the firm to start their own law firm "uptown." They were Skadden, Arps & Slate. Today the successor law firm, Skadden, Arps, Slate, Meagher & Flom, is the biggest (962 lawyers — November 11, 1988) and the richest firm, now earning gross revenues of more than $400,000,000 annually. The change, in a few years, is breathtaking.

It is somehow amazing that annual revenues of the 100 highest-grossing law firms [1987 figures] in the United States totaled over *seven billion dollars.* In another year, this gross figure for these 100 law firms rose by $3.5 *billion* more.

* * *

These transformations are more dramatic when we glance at the law practice of lawyers practicing law — not long ago—when America became a nation. Say, John Marshall, Patrick Henry or Alexander Hamilton. In those days, lawyers practiced law on their own and represented clients on a one-to-one basis. Even in the 1850s, Abraham Lincoln, although a member of a two-partner law firm, was representing clients on a one-to-one basis.

Law partnerships did not appear until the second decade of the 18th century. Founding partners selected their associates and partners. The touchstones were trust, confidence and competence. Until 1900, one leading New York City law firm never had more than five partners.

Not until the 20th century did law *firms* begin to represent clients. This basic realignment in the practice of law provided the seed bed for the present frenzied drive to the business ethos and away from traditional aspirations.

Once the lawyer was no longer representing clients on a one-to-one basis, the law firm took on a life of its own, much the way the corporation started to flourish at the turn of the century as a separate entity. Partners in these new firms find themselves in a somewhat paralyzed posture, as if they had lost independent control.

The giant law firm in America has become an institution in itself. Lawyers in big firms are no longer accountable, for the most part, to individual clients as they used to be. Rather, they are accountable to their law firm's management committee. Law firms are the entity, not the individual. The objective of today's giant law firm is essentially to make money and to grow bigger in order to make more money.

To a large extent the client has been left out in the cold and is beginning to sense, uneasily, the estrangement. Today's big law firm has become an institution for making dollars. The product sold is legal services. Individual representation of individual clients, in the traditional mold, has faded away.

The lawyer in today's giant law firm has a prime obligation to the "firm" — to bill a certain level of collectible hours, to make money, to market wares, to solicit new clients. The lawyer may not say, with impunity, in these megaLawFirms that he or she would prefer to practice as the canons of professional responsibility are presumed to dictate.

Defenders of the giant firm argue that, despite lack of traditional professionalism, the large corporations need the legal assistance, often internationally, of the giant law firm. While there is some merit in this view, the lawyers providing this large business advice need not be deemed "professionals," but rather can serve as well in the more realistic role of "technician", certified as expert in his or her field of practice and subject to less demanding obligations. (This is discussed in Chapter X). At the same time, the large corporation (particularly its chief executive officer and directors) will still most likely need the thoughtful counsel of the professional generalist. In addition to this professional generalist, a larger group is needed: the specialist lawyers who can adequately function as technicians. They will not suffer the embarrassment and the hypocrisy of adherence to strict codes of conduct.

* * *

Philosopher Rene Dubos, microbiologist and experimental pathologist who first demonstrated the feasibility of obtaining germ-fighting drugs from microbes, spent the first half of his life looking through a microscope at microbes and the second half of his life looking at human beings. His observations were so true and so eloquent that he won the Pulitzer Prize. He also made some real contributions to our thinking, such as persuading some of us, for example, in a number of personal meetings together, that human nature has not changed perceptably since the Stone Age.

We can look back to different periods of our history and gain insight as to what is going on and what part the law profession played from Greek days, Roman days, the French Revolution, the American Revolution, the Russian Revolution, the days of the Depression in America and the New Deal and the Reagan and Bush Administrations.

Despite extraordinary expansion of numbers of lawyers, numbers of branch offices, numbers of dollar profits, the frenetic energy displayed by the giant firms, still there is the thought somehow that the effort is misguided and lazy. Misguided because the feat does not illuminate the purpose of the law profession. Lazy because the bottom-line mentality refuses to address the hard choices more complex than profitability and numbers. It is harder to articulate goals to enhance the justice system and the public interest with a great cadre of lawyers. There is evidence of lazy indifference to the matters that count and an unwillingness to shoulder the burden of uncertainty engendered whenever we consider what the future will bring — and, more important, what the future should bring.

The first function of the lawyer, according to barrister Lord MacMillan, is to protect the individual from the oppression of the state. Now, if you say that to younger people who are becoming members of the American Bar, they will laugh because they have not seen any hard evidence — any evidence at all — that any lawyer in America is trained, or needs to be trained, to protect the individual from the oppression of the state.

The second role of a lawyer, according to Lord Macmillan, is to give objective, competent advice, for a reasonable fee, to clients who cannot voyage on their own. The relationship is on a one-to-one basis. The client takes the lawyer's advice on the trust and confidence that the lawyer, specially trained, knows what to advise him to do or not to do.

Lord MacMillan said, in a paper read before the Scottish Philosophical Society in Glasgow after World War I, that the law profession by its *nature* cannot be a trade or business. It has to function as a profession, and the keystone is the trust and confidence between the lawyer and the client and *the honor of the lawyer's word among other colleagues, the court and the client.* Without that, there is, he said, no real reason for having a law profession.

As we go along we need, of course, to come to terms with the modern world, to look to the future and adopt methods of dealing with modern problems and needs. That does not mean trampling on basic tenets underlying the profession itself.

Senior Second Circuit Judge J. Edward Lumbard, in *A Conversation with J. Edward Lumbard* (Charles Evan Hughes Press), with no axe to grind, observes:

"Since I left law school we have seen the growth of these enormous law firms . . . the more people you have with you in a venture, the more you have to consult other people and make compromises of your own point of view, and sometimes of your own standards."

Law associates become, in the giant law firms, fungible articles of commerce driven to constant night and weekend work, generating, in treadmill style, the commodity of billable hours.

* * *

Men are by nature hunters. Litigators by nature are more aggressive hunters. The litigation Bar has grown exponentially because for twenty years it has been more and more lucrative. Also, as a form of risky terroristic warfare, it is deemed less dull than routine corporate law or trusts & estates. Less numbing certainly than drafting a trust indenture.

The giant firms have increasingly forced retirement on its older partners, regardless, in many case, of the talent and skills acquired or the good health of the individual lawyer. Some dictate that at 65 out you go—presumably to "make room" for the younger partners. There are variations of the retirement demands but blanket application of forced retirement is not only cruel and wasteful but is also another indication of the efficient machine at its worst. It reminds me of the western African tribes that would bury their old chief while he was still alive. Some of the finest lawyers have in this decade been disposed of by the megaLawFirms. It is also lazy because it allows no discernment, no exception; it is an ukase of totalitarian methodology—the dull bureaucratic machine at work.

* * *

### *The American Law Profession In The Year 2000*

If current trends continue, what about the future? Will the megaLawFirms grow bigger and bigger into a model of The Big Eight Accountants? Will the avarice of the American lawyer go unchecked? Will the attorneys' code of conduct be watered down to allow more elbow room for narcissistic greed? Will the Sherman-like march of the giant law firms continue its invasions of legal territory coast to coast? What of the future of the "law business?"

We must start by making several assumptions. First, that current trends will continue for a dozen years; that the cupidity of the American lawyer will go on unrestrained; that Bar leaders continue to plan seminars at Boca Raton on how to run a law firm as a business and how to solicit a body of high-paying clients. Massive commando-like raids are routinely made on other firms to loot their rainmakers and capture their clients. A sort of internecine warfare. That the American law profession (now over 800,000), views its exclusive franchise as a license to make money with no frustrating attendant obligation to serve the public interest.

Also that the law profession's Model Code of Responsibility and office lawyer discipline will go on being diluted to allow further opportunities for insatiable greed. Finally, that Bar associations, law schools, and judicial conferences will be devoted to rhetoric and lip service but will stop short of reform.

With these dreary assumptions in hand, what can we reasonably expect the law business in the United States to be in the year 2000?

- MegaLawFirms will achieve the pattern, as have accountants, of The Big Eight. The rest of the Bar will be flotsam and jetsam.
- Law firms will be 10 years behind America's accounting firms in governance, recruiting, marketing, soliciting clients, using seminars, and crossing state and national boundaries with branches. Law firms will also be equally behind in their levels of collegiality, civility, and grace.
- At annual meetings, law firms will issue thick loose-leaf books with head shots of "partners" so members can identify each other.
- The ubiquitous computer will be crowned king. Woe unto any lawyer in The Big Eight law firms who falls behind allotted billable hours of work. All lawyers are satisfied that no computer to date can record those lesser qualities such as fidelity, loyalty, honesty, or altruism for that matter. Just numbers in a numbers society. Only the left side of your brain, please.
- The Federal and state governments — prodded by an enraged citizenry — will make punishing, if inept, regulations in a fumbling effort to curb the grip of The Big Eight lawyers' monopoly on the lucrative and mystical practice of law.
- Everyone will learn doublespeak from the lawyers.
- The American Bar will swell to more than one million lawyers, fed by 35,000 new elite admissions annually. After the year 2000 the law profession will insensibly shrink as students, hungry as locusts, opt for more affluent and prestigious pursuits, such as handling lever-

aged buyouts, hostile takeovers or heavy metal commodity trading in the pits of New York and Chicago. Inside information trading (directed clandestinely from Caribbean hideaways) will become a challenging occupation for the brilliant and the young.

- Women lawyers, in evident disgust, will form their own national Bar groups and exclude men from their law firms. Angry mobs will demonstrate in the streets (and newly-named plazas) against real and imagined lawyer chicanery. Courthouses will be picketed and one enters courts as he might a prison or an airline to the eastern Mediterranean. Lawyers at dinner parties will mumble nervously that they are . . . uh . . . businessmen.
- Creative advertising for lawyers and The Big Eight law firms will know no bounds. Highway billboards; neon lights flashing around town; taxi cabs running videos of svelte legal personalities "Big Joe Bradley is a Winner" and stunning statistics on winning unbelievable sums in damage actions by use of novel twists of jurisprudence. Subways will be brought back from insolvency by the glitter of law firm advertising ("Take a Law Card. Your Road to Wealth"). Firms will be advertised like toothpaste, aspirin and deodorant: MegaLawFirm A will advertise its services for obtaining divorces is 40% better than megaLawFirm B; 50% better than megaLawFirm C.
- Lawyer magazines and glitzy scandal sheets will continue to report the ugly scene as the once-heralded American law profession descends down and down unto the seventh circle.

# VI
# *Morals of the Marketplace*

*"Are you not ashamed of heaping up the greatest amount of money, and caring so little about the wisdom and truth and the greatest improvement of the soul?"*

—SOCRATES, 339 B.C.

STUDY OF THE PAST is, in today's world, relegated to the scholar and the schoolboy. Cultural atrophy sets in as suggested by professors-authors Allan Bloom (of Chicago) and E.D. Hirsch, Jr. (of Virginia). But for those still awake, there are incisive insights found in history.

Thucydides, a sensible Greek historian, and Athenian general until exiled in 431 B.C., wrote this in his later years about human nature:

"Since the nature of the human mind does not change any more than the nature of the human body, circumstances swayed by human nature are bound to repeat themselves, and in the same way, unless it is shown to them that such a course in other days ended disastrously. When the reason why a disaster came about is perceived, people will be able to guard against that particular danger."

Thucydides' climax to his penetrating history of the Greeks tells of the disintegration of a great Athenian people after two hundred years of Periclean glory.

Years of fighting and base intrigue against the common good demeaned the spirit and attitudes of individual Athenians. Thucydides shows in one dreadful story how swift the downward process can be. Through the story itself we can learn the tragedy of this awful result of bad shift of *attitude* and *perspective.*

Within the orbit of Athens' now imperial-style control was Melos, an island of no real significance, but one whose people wished to be neutral. Thucydides records the conversation between the envoys of the Athenians and the leaders of Melos.

The Melians pleaded they had done no wrong and to war against them would be unjust. To which the Athenian envoys replied:

"Justice is attained only when both sides are equal. The powerful exact what they can and the weak yield what they must."

The Melians answered: "You ignore justice, and yet it is to your interest, too, to regard it, because if you are ever defeated you will not be able to appeal to it."

To this the Athenians responded: "You must allow us to take the risk of that. Our point is that we want to subjugate you without trouble to ourselves and that this will be better for you also."

*Melians:* "To become slaves?"

*Athenians:* "Well—it will save you from a worse fate."

*Melians:* "You will not consent to our remaining at peace, your friends, but not your allies?"

*Athenians:* "No. We do not want your friendship. It would appear proof of our own weakness, whereas your hatred is proof of our power. Please remember that with you the question is one of self-preservation. We are the stronger."

*Melians:* "Fortune does not always side with the strong. There is hope that if we do our utmost we can stand erect."

*Athenians:* "Beware of hope. Do not be like the common crowd who when visible grounds for hope fail, betake themselves to the invisible, religion and the like. We advise you to turn away from such folly. And may we remind you that in all this discussion you have not advanced one argument *practical* men would use."

Being impractical, the Melians chose to fight the Athenians. They were defeated swiftly by the Athenians who put the men to death and made slaves of the women and children.

In this decline of mind and spirit, Thucydides noted that Athenians no longer disguised the ugliness of their words and deeds. Vices by then were esteemed as virtues. The meaning of words changed. Deceit was shrewdness. Recklessness was held to be courage. And loyalty, moderation, generosity scorned as proofs of weakness; "good will which is the chief element in a noble nature was laughed out of court and vanished." Every man distrusted every other man.

Seeds of evil in the mind hastened the downfall of Athens. Thus ended the power and the glory of mighty Athens's Golden Age.

* * *

The new business orientation today of the law profession has led insensibly to emaciation of the essential trust and confidence between attorney and client. The lawyer today markets legal services to the client who generally is unable to judge the value and merits of such legal services, including the critical decision whether or not the client should be pressed into the trial arena.

Why do so many lawyers today push their clients into battles in court when the clients' best interests may lie in out-of-court mediation and compromise? This is a question worth asking today. Is it "Stir the pot?"

Litigation nowadays is too often endless, mindless, proliferating and exacerbating, a dreadful drain on the client's peace of mind and pocketbook. Even victory can be Pyrrhic. Where the dispute *cannot* be resolved there is, of course, justification for going to trial. It should be a last, not a first, resort.

In *The Art of War,* over 2,500 years ago, Sun Tzu wrote a remarkable manual about *not* waging war in China:

"To fight and conquer in all your battles is not supreme excellence; supreme excellence consists in breaking the enemy's resistance without fighting."

This paper was brought to the attention of the King of Wu who then appointed Sun Tzu his general. For twenty years thereafter, until the death of Sun Tzu and the king, the armies of Wu were victorious over their hereditary enemies. As Sun Tzu proclaimed, "The true object of war is *peace.*" (He told the king that his rules as set forth were also applicable to every aspect of life's struggles—even including household relations!)

The trial lawyer often becomes a contestant to his own client. Retired United States Army General William Westmoreland retained a trial lawyer in the recent CBS libel case who evidently had insufficient trial experience to try what was in effect his first case. When the case, in his doubtful view began to fall apart, the General's lawyer, without adequate discussion, copped out of the lawsuit, leaving, some believe, his client and his client's principles, high and dry.

* * *

If a lawyer gives attention to a legal matter in proportion to the profit he expects to realize, the client is the one who suffers. Each legal matter is surely unique and one involving a small amount of money can be as complicated or more complicated than a legal problem involving vast sums.

The businessman's approach is necessarily to expend the

greatest effort for the maximum profit. The professional's approach should be to expend the necessary resources to solve the client's problem, without regard to the lawyer's profits. The difference is essential. Mr. Justice Oliver Wendell Holmes, Jr. once remarked when the American law profession was peaking, a half-century ago: "I should say that one of the good things about the law is that it does not pursue money directly. When you sell goods the price which you seek and your own interests are what you think about in the affair. When you try a case you think about the ways to win it and the interests of your client. In the long run *this affects one's whole habit of mind . . .*"

As the legal profession more and more puts profits first, the client's affairs must necessarily come second—or lower. There can only be one paramount concern.

In addition, the very world of the "elite" law firm has changed. To understand the abrupt transition it is important to observe that in many cases the new breed of marketeering lawyers have purposely retained the *trappings* of the old firm names, the old English panelled decor, the old engraved stationery, the chalk-striped dark grey suits, the British guard ties and the Peal shoes. Retained, too, the false image that under their shell they are still the *elite* firm in the sense of dedicated excellence, when in point of cold fact they no longer are. This is a well-kept secret.

Another related topic at the Bar is how much money the partners will make or how much will be made next year. A young bedazzled partner at a reoriented firm at number One Wall Street was quoted as saying, with wide eyes:

"I'm ecstatic that we're now thinking about where the practice is going and how much *money* we should be making this year."

Why these changes? In part, poor amnesiac leadership.

In part, creeping bad economics. In part, politicization of the law firm, infighting, character assassination, and sordid power struggles, gargantuan expenses rising to exceed current revenue. Huge legal bills, deliberately unpaid by the client, are forced into discount. Bank loans are made against receivables. Per capita partner's take-home pay first rises, then declines. "The big firms aren't [automatic] money machines anymore," argues guru consultant Bradford Hildebrandt.

This is somewhat different from earlier days on Wall Street. Franklin Delano Roosevelt, as a young man out of law school, was invited to work, in the Spring of 1907, at the Carter, Ledyard & Milburn firm for *no* pay (at least for the first year), which he readily accepted for the opportunity and the experience. The offering letter from the law firm:

Mr. F. Roosevelt
135 East 36th Street
New York City

Dear Mr. Roosevelt:

I have talked over with Mr. Ledyard the question of your coming to our office, and I find that we can arrange to have a place for you at such time as you may wish to come here in the autumn, not later than October 1st, preferably a week or so earlier.

In case you come to us the arrangement with you will be the same as we usually make in such cases, that is to say, you will come to us the first year without salary, and after you have been with us for a year we would expect, if you remain, to pay you a salary which, however, at the outset would necessarily be rather small.

Very truly yours,

Edmund L. Baylies

After World War I, New York's McAdoo, Cotton & Franklin (now evolved into 220-lawyer Cahill, Gordon & Reindel), considered new legal recruits from Harvard Law School, class of 1919. The senior partners received a memorandum, circulated within the firm, dated April 23, 1919 which read:

"Mr. Gordon, after investigating the situation at Harvard Law School, feels that the two best men available are Mr. Murphy and Mr. Plindel. They are both Law Review men, standing respectively two and three in the class.

" . . . [W]e should take them at once. I believe we can get them . . . at a salary, to start, of $125 a month."

Fresh law school graduates now command, as noted, upwards of $70,000. a year in New York—a 500 per cent jump in 15 years.

Surely there must be a reasonable middle ground between no pay and obscene pay.

* * *

The fall of Boston's Herrick & Smith is a story of a law firm trying to cope with the pressures of surviving in what became a "legal marketplace", dramatically changed in the last decade. What once was thought in Boston to be a gentleman's profession becomes a highly competitive arena in which firms must battle openly to keep old clients and find new ones.

It also is the saga of a firm that could not solve the *internal anxiety* caused by new realities — problems ranging from how to deal with so-called non-productive partners to developing a better compensation system to reward impatient, aggressive and economically more successful lawyers. Computer numbers daily tell all.

Periodically everyone gets the printout from the computer. What do the *numbers* show this quarter, this month, this week — *today?* The left side of the brain deals with numbers. The right side, ideas and creativity.

Inevitably at the big law firms the left side is exalted; and the right side is shut down as irrelevant.

No large urban firm has been immune from such stresses of fierce economic competition and infighting. But the closing of Herrick & Smith marks the first time an old-line Boston partnership has decided to terminate. And although rumors that the 79-lawyer firm was in trouble as a cohesive firm had been circulating for months, news of its death surprised and dismayed the proud Boston Bar.

Frustrated by the firm's reluctance to change and to deal with what were termed "deadwood" partners who had small billings, higher power lawyers began to leave the firm, of course taking fat clients with them. The bloodletting began.

Partners at Herrick & Smith considered measures to reverse the firm's fortunes. They took a retreat in Newport, R.I. to hear last-minute suggestions from Arthur Young & Co., a national *accounting* firm. More discussions of numbers. As a result, the firm instituted a new compensation system which relied *less* on seniority and *more* on "production," hoping to appease hungry younger partners generating large billings. They say the new system helped ease some tensions, but it did not solve the nagging problem of how to attract new business to the firm.

* * *

I remember in the 1940s a bright boyish professor at Yale Law School, Fred Rodell, who a few years earlier wrote a provocative book, *Woe Unto You Lawyers!* which achieved quick notoriety.

It was Rodell's thesis that the law as espoused by lawyers is a sort of hocus-pocus quasi-science. "In tribal times," Rodell told us, "there were the medicine-men. In the Middle Ages, there were the priests. Today, there are the lawyers. For every age, a group of bright boys, learned in their trade and jealous of their learning, who blend technical competence with plain and fancy hocus-pocus to make themselves masters of their fellow men. For every age, a pseudo-intellectual autocracy, guarding the tricks of its trade from the un-initiated, and running, after its own patterns, the civilization of its day."

The attitude and perspective grows. In 1987, two New York City giant law firms locked horns against each other in an elaborate morality play, a multi-party fraud action (naming one of the law firms as a *defendant!*) all arising out of the Ivan Boesky scandals. Major newspapers splashily announced the opening guns with pages of zippy copy about the *law firms* engaged in battle, about the selected legal team commandos drawn up, and finally columns of type and hype spotlighting the star litigators themselves, glorified and announced like prizefighters.

Homer at Troy would be hard put to compete.

The morals of the marketplace are fitting for the market but not for the legal profession.

# VII

## *Lawyers as Thick as Locusts*

> *"It is worth our while to perceive that the final reason for Rome's {decline and} defeat was the failure of* mind *and* spirit *to rise to a new and great opportunity, to meet the challenge of new and great events. Material development outstripped human development; the Dark Ages took possession of Europe, and classical antiquity ended."*
>
> —EDITH HAMILTON, *The Roman Way*

THE ROMAN BAR was at its height around the time of the birth of Christ. It was, as Gibbon reported, small, educated and dedicated to service of the public interest. Its reputation was a profession devoted to excellence. Most members of its Bar were honorable and, at that time, expected to be.

Gibbon, an 18th Century observer, saw no pejorative slur in referring to this Bar as "patrician." But what evidence exists indicates that the members of this Bar performed services of high quality and avoided the soft porn shoulders of greed and self-aggrandizement.

One example of this high-minded Roman law professional is Marcus Tullius Cicero.

Some years before Cicero's headless body was found along the Italian seashore, he was an eloquent leader of the Roman Bar, a learned man given to writing letters, many of which survive.

Cicero had his political differences which, in those turbulent Roman days, had fierce consequences, worse than death, such as being *exiled* from Rome to the hinterlands.

In 57 B.C., Cicero was back in Rome after a deadening period of exile to find to his joy a retainer to try what became a celebrated murder case, with all the intriguing subplots and nuances that would bring the trial, even today, to the forefront of the tabloids and perhaps television's Masterpiece Theater, felicitously narrated by Alastair Cooke.

A well-known aristocratic beauty brought a bombshell charge of murder and attempt to poison against one of the most brilliant young elegants in Rome. The two had been intimate lovers. For a time, dodging the husband, the lovers had lived and frolicked at her grand house overlooking the Tiber.

Now they faced each other in the crowded festival-spirited trial forum—the accuser Clodia, once Cicero's friend, and the accused, represented by Cicero, a delightful, if cynical, young man, Caelius Rufus.

Clodia, dressed to the nines, took her place in the front row. Ladies of fashion and all the wits of the town arrived early for favorable seats. This scandal would be electric theatre and Rome's society loved it all. Clodia was known to have numerous trysts with all sorts of persons, including a sweet one with the poet Catallus whose delicate love poems to her had brought her, perhaps undeservedly, a kind of immortality.

Now at the opening of the trial, more intense and moving than Claus von Bulow's, Clodia is seated disdainfully superior in her indifference to the sneers of lesser Roman folk around her. Clodia's brother, a power in the city as a descendant of Claudius, was a bitter foe, it so happened, of Cicero and had gone so far as to manage his recent exile from Rome.

The defendant Caelius Refus, ten years younger than the imperious Clodia and twenty years less experienced, was obviously nervous. The charges against him were devastating. If proved, he would be ruined. It may have occurred to him that he had acted foolishly when, wearied of an older woman's passion, he had dumped her, perhaps unceremoniously, for other interests on the other side of town.

He may at that point have regretted his laughing at her advances and his ungracious habit of getting Romans to laugh as well. He had called her in the taverns "Quadrantaria," the lady whose price is a penny. The taunt roamed through the city.

Caelius Refus was sensibly in a state of fear and looked to the skill of his lawyer as his only chance of escape.

The prosecution began. Caelius Refus had hired agents to assassinate the envoy of the king of Egypt with money Clodia had given him. With some of this money he had bribed slaves to poison Clodia. Solemn suborned witnesses swore to both charges.

Cicero, well prepared and well trained, rose to defend. As a Roman citizen and an educated observer of the assembled crowd, he knew, as if instinctively, the notes to play and the subtle wending way to acquittal.

Without artifice, his voice confiding, he spoke to the judges and jury and the assembled mob of spectators. A stunning spectacle was reaching a climax:

"The whole case, gentlemen of the jury, rests upon Clodia, a woman known not only by her noble birth but by the crowd's complete familiarity with her [laughter].

"I wish I need not name her, the more that there has been enmity between me and her husband — I mean, her brother. I am always making that mistake — [ripples of laughter from the crowd, well aware of the scandal of Clodia's relations with her brother].

"And, indeed, I never thought to take upon me a quarrel with a woman, especially with one who far from being considered any man's adversary is universally held to be the intimate of all [laughter].

"I would not offend her. Let me ask her how she would prefer me to address her—in the grave, old-fashioned style or in the lighter manner of today? If the first, I must summon one to rise from the dead, that grand old blind man, of all her family the most renowned, not sorry today that he cannot see who sits before him. He shall stand here and speak in my stead:

" 'Clodia, what have you to do with Caelius? How is it that you were so intimate with him as to give him money, or so hostile to him as to fear to be poisoned by him? You, your father's daughter, the descendant of generations of men who were Rome's consuls, the wife of a man Rome delighted to honor—why did you seek this intimacy? Was he your husband's friend—was he related to you by blood or by marriage?

" 'None of these, O daughter of a house where the women have ever equalled the men in glorious renown. Did I break off a base peace with Rome's bitter foe that you might enter into an alliance of a shameful love? Did I bring water to the city for you to wash away your filthiness? Did I build the great highway that you might take your pleasure on it with strange men?'

"But perhaps, Clodia, you prefer me to speak to you as a man of the world? Let me dispose of that stern, rugged figure and choose as my spokesman, most appropriately, that perfect man of the world, your youngest brother, who loves you very much. He asks you what all this to-do is about. 'Are you out of your head, sister, making such a molehill into a mountain? You took a fancy to the young man next door — to his handsome face and figure. His father gave him little money; you tried to bind him to you with some of yours.

" 'But he found he must pay too high for your gifts and he has done with you. What of it? Are there no others? Those gardens of yours by the Tiber which you have fitted up so that all the young men want to take their swim there — what is the use of them if you cannot pick and choose as you want? Why make yourself a nuisance to someone who does not want you?' "

Cicero then turns to his client. "And yet, gentlemen of the jury, we ourselves can remember the hot youth of some among us today. Understand me, gentlemen, I have no intention of naming anyone, but if I had, you will bear me out, I should have no trouble.

"To speak plain truth, if any woman throws her house open to whosoever desires, if without disguise she leads a courtesan's life, if she acts here in the city, in her gardens, at Baiae, that what she is apparent not only by her gait, her dress, her burning eyes, her freedom of speech, but by such entertainments as only women of that kind offer, would you judge a young man who approached her guilty of wrong or merely bent on a moment's pleasure?

"Tell me, Clodia, would a man who had intercourse with that sort of woman — completely unlike yourself, of course [laughter] be disgraced and degraded in your eyes? If you are not such a one, as I grant you, how could Caelius act with you as he is said to have done? If you are, your life makes null and void any testimony from you."

At this point Cicero, his voicc rising and mocking in tone, turns to the charge of poison:

"Gentlemen of the jury, I saw — I myself saw and with

as bitter pain as I ever felt in my life, the excellent Metellus, this lady's husband, dying, him whom the day before I had met in the Senate house, enjoying the full strength of his vigorous prime. I saw him struggling to speak, his voice choked with agony, striking the wall in his paroxysms. From that house Clodia comes and dares to speak of the effect of swift poison?"

With this final thrust, Cicero closed his summation. The two charges of Clodia, he said, rested on nothing of substance, no rational argument, no conclusion necessitated by the premises, but only on the words of witnesses everyone knew were hireable at any crossroad of the city for any statement desired.

The quick verdict vindicated Caelius and equally condemned Clodia for her perfidy. The advocacy of Cicero—intelligent and human,—saved the young man from a hellish fate.

# PART FOUR

## *VIII. The Lawyer Monopoly: The Exclusive Franchise*

## *IX. Roots of Law Practice*

*"File and forget. We always have good reasons for doing* nothing."

—SMILEY IN JOHN LE CARRE'S *The Honorable Schoolboy.*

# VIII
## *The Lawyer Monopoly: The Exclusive Franchise*

*"A basic tenet of the professional responsibility of lawyers is that every person in our society should have ready access to the independent professional services of a lawyer of integrity and competence."*

—Model Code of Professional Responsibility.

IF THE BAR wants to remain independent, and govern itself by special rules of conduct, it must be clear that independence and those special rules are not arrogant masks for self-opportunism and greed. If the Bar wants to keep its monopoly on the delivery of legal services, the profession must show that it will provide legal services of quality competently and objectively at reasonable cost to all those who need them, on all levels of our society.

Sir Francis Bacon understood that "the greatest trust between man and man is the trust of giving counsel." (Later in his career, Sir Francis forgot this nugget of wisdom and ended up, after conviction for accepting bribes on the bench, in the Tower of London). Out of this particular attorney-client relationship springs a quite different — and special — set of values, standards, and prescriptions.

These considerations — based on the experience of centuries — have been hammered into codes, canons, customs, and traditions that seek to assure that the law profession faithfully serves its critical functions.

Whitney North Seymour, Sr. once remarked that the "breadth of the lawyer's obligations does not rest alone on logic. No lawyer who tries to serve the public interest through the organized bar or otherwise, first says to himself: 'I must do this to justify my exclusive franchise.' "

"Rather his sense of professional and public responsibility is an almost *instinctive by-product of his whole background and training for the profession.* With good luck, he is nourished on it from the moment he chooses the profession; the great law teachers, who themselves chose the profession because it was much more than a way to make a living, *weave the sense of duty into their teaching,* and many lawyers and judges emphasize it in their lives."

To measure decline of the legal profession there must be some knowledge of the standards and examples of earlier days of the profession, yet we must remember that traditions and insights learned in the past do not mean a life at the Bar lived or relived in the past. *We live and practice in the modern day present, but we look always to the future. No successful law profession can emerge and be sustained without being an inspiration for the future.*

Leonard S. Janofsky, past president of the American Bar Association, spoke of a lawyer's paramount obligation at a Bar meeting in Los Angeles: "Of course, we have a right to earn a living, a right to charge a fee, and even a right to advertise our services. But *before any right,* we have an obligation. That our obligation comes first, is what makes us professional."

Henry L. Stimson, a lawyer of note, once said in the introduction to his book (with McGeorge Bundy), On *Active Service in War and Peace,* "Through many channels I came to learn and understand the noble history of the profession of the law. I came to realize that without a Bar trained in the traditions of courage and loyalty our constitutional theories of individual liberty would cease to be a living reality.

"I learned of the experience of those many countries possessing Constitutions and Bills of Rights similar to our own, whose citizens had nevertheless lost their liberties because they did not possess a Bar with sufficient courage and independence to establish those rights by a brave assertion of the writs of habeas corpus and certiorari.

"So I came to feel that the American lawyer should regard himself as a potential officer of his government and a defender of its laws and Constitution. *I felt that if the time should ever come when this tradition had faded out and the members of the Bar had become merely the servants of business, the future of our liberties would be gloomy indeed.*"

Henry L. Stimson never sought public office, yet served under six presidents and in the cabinets of four, including Secretary of War under Franklin Delano Roosevelt. Stimson is responsible for training a cadre of great lawyers who carry on to this day.

* * *

Many good and able people today ask why the law profession's descent to business is necessarily bad for the profession. The reason may be that the lawyer's monopolistic license to practice law stems from commitment to public service. This includes helping out in the community and also protecting individuals from oppression of the state.

The Argentinian newspaper publisher, Jacobo Timerman, was jailed incommunicado and tortured in 1977 for speaking out against the fascistic and repressive junta.

"At dawn, one morning," Timerman tells us — "some 20 civilians besieged my apartment in midtown Buenos Aires. They said they were obeying orders from the 10th Infantry Brigade of the First Army Corps. They covered my head with a blanket. They threw me in the back of the car . . . ."

A lawyer, Genaro Carrio, came to Timerman's wife, at great personal and professional risk, and said that he would be willing to go to the courts to free her husband. Timerman's wife replied that she had no money to pay him since their property had been impounded. The Argentinian lawyer said, "I will do this work without fee." And he did and Jacobo Timerman was eventually released.

* * *

David Margolick reports the horrible ordeal of a Korean greengrocer, Kyroon Ahn, wrongfully charged in Brooklyn Criminal Court with assault and harassment stemming from a fierce squabble with a customer in his store. In fact, the customer had abused and assaulted the greengrocer. Such ethnic and racial tensions are common in changing urban neighborhoods.

The greengrocer Kyroon Ahn, who could not speak enough English to explain, was taken away in handcuffs by the police and booked without an opportunity even to lock his store. When he returned, hours later, it had been looted. A neighborhood foot patrolman heard about the injustice and found a lawyer, Richard Guay, who agreed to represent the greengrocer without his usual fee.

Although offered opportunity to his client to plead guilty to a lesser *criminal* charge, defense lawyer Guay rejected the plea. "I was sent into the case so my client would walk away with dignity," he explained, "not to be processed by the criminal system and plead guilty to some reduced charge for the sake of expediency."

So he filed a petition asking the court to dismiss the case.

The Brooklyn district attorney's office stubbornly opposed. Client Kyroon Ahn next learned — with immense relief—that his lawyer had succeeded and the case was dismissed by the court.

By accepting the monopoly of practicing law, the lawyer should be committed to service of the public interest.

# IX

## *Roots of Law Practice*

*"No great improvements in the lot of mankind are possible until a great change takes place in their mode of thought."*

—JOHN STUART MILL

ARTHUR TRAIN, writing about *The Adventures of Ephraim Tutt,* suggested that the famous main character lawyer, Mr. Tutt, was "certainly not of the firm of Howe & Hummel [rough and tumble] on the one hand nor was he John L. Cadwalader on the other [smooth]." Train then said:

"I have known lawyers, usually old-timers—not unlike him in many ways, for the law offers greater opportunities to be at one and the same time a [gentleman] and a horse trader, than any other profession. Spiritually I suppose that Mr,. Tutt is a combination of most of the qualities which I would like to have, coupled with a few that are common to all of us. One critic has disposed of him by saying that his popularity is due to the fact that he's a hodge-podge of Puck, Robin Hood, Abraham Lincoln and Uncle Sam."

Looking at the practice of law at the turn of the last century, I found a yellowed clipping from the Philadelphia newspaper about a dinner given in 1909 for William Francis Johnson by 150 judges and lawyers.

They had come together to compliment a living senior, as the newspaper clipping said, "not because he had got some new power by election or appointment but just because he was a lawyer, just because he had lived a long honorable career, setting a high example of courtesy, a high example of learning and eloquence, but above all, because he always had a cheerful word for his fellows and had never been backward about putting his hand of encouragement upon an associate's shoulder when he was down on his luck."

Is something lost when cynicism and avarice comes forth as the bannerflag of a new kind of Bar? Lawyer Orville Schell, who died in 1987, thought so. He managed with great leadership the 180-lawyer Hughes Hubbard & Reed firm, headed the Association of the Bar of the City of New York and led a delegation of lawyers on an effective anti-Vietnam war crusade to Washington, D.C.

"There's scarcely been a time when I haven't been on the lookout for clients," Orville Schell once said. "But when people running the big firms throw down the concept of fraternity and collegiality, they fling away their birthright."

The shifting in lawyers' attitude and outlook has been subtle, but the impact is great. I suspect that some members of the Bar are content with the breakdown of standards as it allows them license to do as they please for their own benefit.

Many Bar leaders have been discrete about the havoc, if not silent. Few complain. At a lawyer's seminar at a posh Florida hotel the agenda had been devoted to business techniques to build a firm's law practice. The moderator was a well-regarded former Attorney General of the United States. After the meeting, he acknowledged with a shrug, "the law profession is now a business and there is not much that can be done about it", pointing at the "standing room only" attendance at the lawyers' Boca Raton "business orientation seminar."

A recent Attorney General of the United States, Edwin

Meese 3rd, speaking in New York City in a crowded roon of business people—within a magnificent club on Fifth Avenue founded by J. P. Morgan—began his address, after his troubled confirmation by the Congress, with an insipid joke about how lawyers defraud clients by submission of legal bills with padded time. The whole room rocked with laughter at his clever humor. The decline of lawyer integrity was being cheerfully accepted as conventional wisdom.

* * *

Roots of law practice go back thousands of years and have grown stronger through experience. These basic professional roots should be nurtured, not ignored or severed. There is more chance that these fundamental legal roots will be nurtured if lawyers would reflect on their origins and purpose. In this way, discussion and understanding can pave the way to a fairer, more civilized society.

# Part Five

## X. *Separate the Bar to Save the Profession*

## XI. *Restoring Collegiality and Grace to the Profession: A Sampler*

## XII. *Conclusion: What Can Be Done?*

*"Under the First Amendment there is no such thing as a false idea. However pernicious an idea may seem, we depend for its correction not on the conscience of judges and juries but on the competition of other ideas."*

—Mr. Justice Lewis F. Powell, Jr.

# X
# *Separate the Bar to Save the Profession*

*"We must follow the example of Solon, who gave the Athenians not the best government he could devise but the best they would receive."*

—PIERCE BUTLER, South Carolina delegate to the Constitutional Convention, 1787

SHOULD SELFISH TRENDS continue in their current downgrade course, the American legal profession could be compelled to separate into two groups. The remedy would be simple in execution—although high resistance can be expected from lawyers:

Those lawyers directly involved in the administration of our judicial system, who can demonstrate to state Bar commissions their ability and willingness to abide by strict professional standards as "officers of the court" would be licensed by the state as "Counsellors-at-Law."

This smaller segment of the Bar — approximately 80,000 nationwide — would in effect become the "law profession" on which the public can reasonably rely for professional service.

The balance of the existing Bar who forego practice in our judicial system or who are unwilling or unable to meet the requisite high professional standards of conduct, would remain as "Attorneys-at-Law."

Counsellors-at-law and attorneys-at-law, the proposed separated entities of the American Bar, would be monitored closely by their own local and state Bar associations which set appropriate standards in accordance with function and purpose. Standards for counsellors-at-law will be higher; standards for attorneys-at-law, lower.

This proposal is less a radical departure in the law profession than a benign recognition that this is largely the reality of today.

Although there would be two groups providing legal services, I am not in any sense suggesting that what would result in this country would be in any way comparable to the British system of barristers and solicitors.

There, in a totally different climate, in England and Wales, barristers are a handful; at the 1986 court there were 5,494 in practice, of whom 558 were Queen's Counsel. Under the procedures in England and Wales, barristers deal generally with the larger and significant lawsuits and with more serious criminal cases, although solicitors have blanket access to the Crown Court (criminal cases) and strictly limited access to the High Court (civil cases).

Judges in the High Court are drawn from the ranks of barristers, usually from the ranks of Queen's Counsel. The rest of the lawyering, including much of the court work in Magistrate's Courts and County Courts, is done by solicitors, of whom there are, at recent count (in 1987), over 64,000.

In Scotland (which has its own separate legal system), the pattern is much the same, although the numbers are much lower because the population of Scotland is small. In Scotland, a barrister is known as an "advocate."

The British Bar does not appear, in any sense, to have suffered the downfalls of its American cousins' Bar, although today we hear rumblings of changes in the wings. Between the two there are virtually no valid comparisons.

After two centuries, the American law profession, warts and all, is now indigenous to its native soil.

This professional surgery of separating the American Bar may be forced upon the lawyers if the legal profession continues to decline in its responsibility.

A crucial issue soon to be faced is whether the citizens of America will continue to allow the lawyers uninvolved in the administration of its judicial system, or attorneys-at-law as I have described them, to continue their monopoly in the form of exclusive license to provide legal service for fees set by themselves.

In absence of any real public service by these lawyers, citizens may ultimately force them, through the acts of higher courts and state legislators, to give up their monopolistic license and instead be *certified* merely as paid legal specialists, which, after all, is what they are.

What can be done in the context of character and fitness requirements for entry into the law profession is complex because the observable faults lie primarily in the entrants' mind, not in the printout of college grades.

How do you inculcate, or calculate, altruism, honor or character about a law student? We could have teaching in the law schools about the origins, nature and the history of the profession.

The profession, in any event, never should be closed or handicapped to anyone, by reason of race, creed, color, sex or ethnic background. The standards for entry must be based on excellence in the true sense and the attitudinal discipline to serve rather than to get.

The most positive development in the past twelve years has been the flow of minority students and women into the law profession. Affirmative recruiting by large and small law firms has admirably accounted for the minorities influx, while the law firms' new willingness to hire and promote women has accounted for their joining the Bar.

Milbank, Tweed, Hadley & McCloy announced an historic event—a double winner—election of a black woman to partnership in the 1987 rounds, Patricia Irvin, became the first black partner at the firm. "It has nothing to do with sex or race," defensively stated firm chairman Alexander Forger. "She is a super corporate lawyer." Patricia Irvin, popular with everyone, works 70 to 80 hours a week and at the same time is one of the most active Milbank lawyers in *pro bono* and public service work.

The future success of the Bar depends critically on these conditions for becoming a member of the law profession and thus an instrument for furthering justice in the United States.

* * *

Many things can also be done that seem at first of little consequence. As Pascal noted, little things affect us because little things afflict us. Not all beneficence need be grand. For one sample, what can be done to assist restoration of *grace* and *collegiality* of the Bar? A moment's thought, a moment's caring, perhaps a conversation, giving time (perhaps) to the enlightenment of new entries to the Bar.

# XI

## *Restoring Collegiality and Grace to the Profession: A Sampler*

JUST ONE SMALL sample suggestion is based on the concept of each lawyer taking his or her time to try in daily ways to remedy the current problem of warped attitude and myopic outlook on what the law profession is about. Conveyance of the message can often be accomplished in a relaxed atmosphere.

When Learned Hand was still active on the Second Circuit Court of Appeals, he and District Judge Edward J. Weinfeld would occasionally eat together at a lunch counter near Foley Square.

One day Hand's colleague Judge John Marshall Harlan was appointed to the United States Supreme Court. Judges Hand and Weinfeld invited Harlan to join them for lunch.

When they arrived at the lunch counter, Judge Weinfeld said to the young black man behind the counter, "Say hello to the next Justice of the United States Supreme Court." The young fellow came around from behind the counter, stuck out his hand and said:

"I'm proud to shake the hand of the grandson of the man who wrote the dissent in *Plessy v. Ferguson.*" [a landmark dissent to segregation of blacks].

That story is one that some trial lawyers enjoy telling and hearing because it is true; it is entertaining; and it tells a lot about the quality of our bench.

Trial lawyers are storytellers by nature. The best jury summation is a good story told well.

Put two veteran advocates together in a relaxed setting and each will try to outdo the other with anecdotes about judges, juries, witnesses or clients.

Swapping tales is not only the hallmark of the trial lawyer, it is also the key to the collegiality of the trial bar. Litigators like each other's company primarily because of the stories they tell.

Is it possible this tradition may be dying out?

In early New York, a student of the law could aspire to two professional certificates: one, the initial license to practice as Attorney-at-Law (office practice), and the second, Counsellor-at-Law, granted only after his elders found him "able" and "honest", permitting him to appear and try cases in higher courts.

Nowadays the two licenses are lazily combined, as evidenced by our highest appellate tribunal, the Supreme Court of the United States, where one's admission is as "Attorney and Counsellor."

Young lawyers at large firms are well paid today; some earn more than Federal judges. No one can deny that these young men and women work incredible hours for their monetary rewards. Yet, in focusing on billable hours and financial advancement, these lawyers have little, if any time left to contemplate the general philosophy and traditions of the practice of law. (Ilan Reich, the rich firm lawyer sentenced to jail by Judge Sweet, was touted by his own lawyer to the judge as having annual "*billing* between 2,700 and 3,000" hours to achieve the status of partner. How could he possibly have had time for other than the grindstone of legal work and sending out bills to clients? This is a sad loss.)

There was a day, within memory, when the relationship between the older and younger members of the American Bar was close. Young trial associates would literally follow their seniors about. They saw; they listened; they learned—more than just common law, statutes, and procedures.

One day over lunch recently, several litigators were lamenting this state of affairs and came up with the idea of holding a small dinner twice a year at a place with a good kitchen and wine cellar, where they could spend the evening together telling anecdotes of courtroom triumphs (and trumps) and stories about colorful trial judges.

The novel ingredient was that each veteran would invite a younger lawyer or law student, pointed toward trial practice, as a personal dinner guest, thereby providing a fresh audience for the storytelling, and passing the torch on to future litigators.

So far there have been nine semi-annual "Advocates Dinners," and next year's are already booked.

The concept of the advocates dinners was directly appropriated from the British Inns of Court tradition, where eating a specified number of dinners with one's elders is a mandatory part of preparing for admission to the trial bar. The Advocates dinners are simpler and less formal.

Anecdotes recalled over dinner have ranged from tales of ancient Greece and Rome to current scandals of urban municipal corruption. Titans of the litigation Bar who have figured in the stores include Thomas Erskine, Charles Dickens (former court reporter), Daniel Webster, Benjamin N. Cardozo, Louis Brandeis, John W. Davis, Emory Buckner, Learned Hand, William Donovan, R. Keith Kane, John Marshall Harlan, Max Steuer, Theodore Kiendl, David W. Peck, J. Edward Lumbard, and other legendary figures of the bench and bar. This is the stuff that gives substance and pride to an old calling. And implicit in these exchanges is the more complete education of the young entry into the profession of law.

Finally, we can consider what further practical action can be carried out to save the American law profession from further disintegration caused by the current selling, or selling out, of the profession by many rascals—or innocent persons who perhaps don't know the consequences of what they are doing.

# XII

## *Conclusion: What Should Be Done?*

WHAT CAN BE DONE to resurrect and rejuvenate the American law profession now in serious decline?

- Separate the Bar into Counsellors-at-Law (licensed) and Attorneys-at-Law (unlicensed but certified for expertise.) A smaller, higher-standard professional cadre can perform responsibilities which the current huge Bar of almost a million have not, and probably will not, perform. The move to separate the profession must come largely from the layperson, as a host of lawyers, happy as they are selling the profession, will most likely refuse to budge.
- Recognize that the law profession is in trouble and its monopolistic license endangered by the incessant undermining of the traditional practice of law to become just another business. The unique function and purpose of the profession necessitates that the American law practice be in the service of the public interest.
- Stop the current habit of lawyers stirring up conflicts to create and exacerbate for themselves new and lucrative legal business. Insist that those licensed in the law profession act to resolve disputes by means other than litigation by scorched-earth warfare. Going into the trial arena should be a last resort. Professional lawyers must be healers, not procurers.
- Introduce into the lawyers' Code of Professional Responsibility that lawyers are in fact "officers of the court," responsible to be an instrument to enhance—

day to day—America's justice system in all its myriad forms. Lawyers who are not officers of the court (and act as if they were not) should have their licenses lifted. There are other things to do.

- Lawyers should pledge that members of the Bar will treat colleagues professionally and courteously. Professional courtesy actually invigorates advocacy.
- Law professors should take up a firmer participation in actively grooming more qualified legal professionals who are equipped ethically to carry on a high professional role. They should report to law school authorities relevant information bearing on the character of the student of law.
- Character and integrity cannot be quantified on a computer but are essential to the fabric of all professionalism. Stop using the computer as the sole source of hiring, promoting and firing. It is stupid, incomplete and inhumane as well.
- Lawyers should cease spending time and energy on management techniques, marketing and technology. Necessity does not require discarding centuries of professionalism. What the profession needs most is leadership and inspiration, not management.
- Regardless of later specialization in various areas of the law, lawyers should consciously and voluntarily broaden their own general education, particularly in the humanities throughout their whole career. A narrow, formal education and a narrow specialty produce a narrow-minded person unfit to act as counsellor-at-law.
- Bar members should maintain their own vigilant self-policing system. Lawyers should be intelligent enough and mature enough to enforce their own codes and rules.

- If the American law profession does not do its duty in the public interest, the administration of justice and the aspirations of the profession, then its trust will be taken away and public regulation will soon be making decisions which the profession should be making for itself.
- Law schools and law firms should recognize that cut-throat competition for school grades is corrupting to education and personal growth. Benno C. Schmidt, Jr., Yale's President, said at his introduction (before his induction) that in educating and recruiting law schools and law firms should place greater emphasis on values of judgment, altruism, mutual respect and helpfulness in measuring admission *and* promotion.

Yale's new president put it clearly: "See that all legal institutions value not only excellence in scholarship, but also strength of character, personal grace and moral force."

## *Coda*

*WE THE PEOPLE of the United States, in Order to form a more perfect Union, establish Justice,* insure domestic Tranquility, provide for the common defense, promote the general Welfare, and secure the Blessings of Liberty to ourselves and our Posterity, do ordain and establish this Constitution for the United States of America.

—PREAMBLE

NO SOCIETY, or profession for that matter, goes backwards, nor can it live with sense and vitality in the past. History is past experience but it can teach how to live in the future.

The troubling question remains how well we have achieved the goal set forth in the preamble of our Constitution of the establishment of Justice. Too significant a portion of the American Bar in the last decade has ignored or resisted its professional obligation to enhance the justice system.

What can be done by Americans—lawyers and non-lawyers alike—to restore the law profession to its fundamental role as a cadre for preserving our justice system and, in turn, our civilization?

*The Douglas Letters,* published in late 1987, offer glimpses of how William O. Douglas (who retired from the Supreme Court in 1975, after serving over 36 years, with a reputation as a defender of individual liberties) had this to say in a letter to young lawyers. He wrote that the Constitution and the Bill of Rights "guarantee to us all the rights to personal and spiritual self-fulfillment. "But," Douglas said, "the guarantee is not self-executing." Then he added, "As nightfall does not come at once, neither does oppression. In both instances, there is a twilight when everything remains *seemingly* unchanged. And it is in such twilight that we all must be most aware of *change* in the air—however slight—lest we become unwitting victims of the darkness."

American lawyers must be urged to become strong instruments to advance the ends of justice and to stop the selling of the profession.

# *Author's Personal Note*

## *Confrontation About the Changing Nature of the Law Profession*

In writing of the marked decline of the American law profession, I have thought, in fairness, I owe the reader a brief account of a professional confrontation on the key issue whether the law is really a profession, which resulted in an attempt by a newly-elected management committee to oust me from a large Wall Street law firm.

Few law firms could claim the illustrious history and performance, since 1792, of Cadwalader, Wickersham & Taft. That was the year John Wells, who escaped as a child from the Cherry Valley Indian massacre in upstate New York, was admitted to practice in New York as an "attorney-at-law."

By 1795 the founder of this seminal law firm was admitted in New York as a "counsellor-at-law" (barrister) having passed muster for "ability" and "honor", allowing trial practice in New York's higher courts.

Wells rose swiftly to become a leading trial lawyer in young America, renowned for his eloquence and character. Among his friends were Alexander Hamilton, James Madison and Aaron Burr. Their mutual interests extended beyond the techniques of the law to ripening political life and the arcane philosophy of human nature.

In 1818 John Wells formed one of the first law partnerships with George Washington Strong. Wells worked in the courts; Strong worked in the office on Wall Street. It was a happy and prosperous practice.

By the end of the nineteenth century the Wells & Strong

firm had established itself, both here and abroad, as highly competent and professional. Strong's son, George Templeton Strong, wrote a diary of this period in New York (1835 – 1875) that records the turbulence and heroics, on all levels of life, during these times as well as details of the firm's law practice. (Some of these diaries have been published; Louis Auchincloss calls them a singular contribution to American literature). By 1900 the firm had six partners, probably as large a number as any firm at that time.

John Lambert Cadwalader came over to New York from Philadelphia before the Civil War with a letter from his father addressed to "Daniel Lord, Esq." testifying that his son "has a good hand and he has never given me any trouble." Later, in the Grant Administration, young Cadwalader served as Assistant Secretary of State under Hamilton Fish; their public office was a fine building housing several people located in those days next to the White House. After a trip around the world, Cadwalader joined the Strong firm, which by 1913 would become Cadwalader, Wickersham & Taft.

All three name partners, with significant international practice, were recognized as distinguished lawyers, and generous and able public servants. All three were presidents of the Association of the Bar of the City of New York, formed in 1870 by spirited leaders of the Bar to curb notorious municipal corruption. (Today this tradition has been carried on by high-minded presidents such as Herbert Brownell, Cyrus Vance, Robert M. Kaufman and Sheldon Oliensis).

George W. Wickersham was, for a period, Attorney General of the United States and Henry Taft, a gifted barrister and writer, was a brother of the President. Wickersham is credited with proposing the great Learned Hand for a Federal judgeship in New York.

Under their leadership and example, the law firm flourished for decades. The Cadwalader firm for all these years set a moral and professional tone for the Bar as a whole. It became the measure of what was done in law practice and, more important, what was not done.

In the Fall of 1955, a senior partner of the firm R. Keith Kane invited me down for an interview. His reputation preceded him—president of his Harvard Class, captain of its top football team, successful, humane counsellor-at-law and notable public servant. He introduced me to the presiding partner ("the General"), Cornelius W. Wickersham, son of George W. Wickersham; to Jacquelin (Jack) Swords, who was designing a litigation arm for the firm; H. Lee White, who had served with distinction in the Air Force and was now a leader in the international shipping field, and H. Gilmore Wells, a personable tax specialist. Also to Robert Lee and his wife Catherine, one of the first lady law partners on Wall Street; and to F. Sims McGrath, (author of "Pillars of Maryland") whose daughter Peggy married David Rockefeller.

They told me that the firm had somewhat faltered during the five-year interruptions of World War II and its aftermath, and currently, led by Kane and Swords, was undergoing a dynamic resurgence. Jack Swords suggested I become his assistant in his effort to create a litigation team. He had been spending about half his time in the estates and trusts field while his real interest was in the trial and appeal of law cases.

In a few days I received an offer from the General to come on board as an associate. I quickly accepted and this began a professional relationship and exciting work for the next quarter century.

By 1982 — 27 years later — all of these eight leading partners of the Cadwalader firm had died. The firm had grown from 55 lawyers in 1955 to 170 lawyers with offices in New York City, Washington, D.C. and Palm Beach, Florida — a total crew of over 450 persons. A new elected management committee of five was installed after an interminable and intriguing campaign for votes.

A new mood had settled in, of tension and uncertainty as to new goals, new procedures and new values.

Once in power, the new managers sent out impersonal memoranda which, in rapid fire, removed me as head of the litigation group, one of the largest and most lucrative departments of the firm, dismissed me as chairman of the ethics committee, reduced my share of profits and then summoned me to a meeting with the five new managers on Tuesday, March 23.

It was no surprise that this would be a confrontation, brewing for several years, essentially over a difference of opinion about the nature and conduct of a professional law firm.

For the previous three years at meetings, public and private, I had been trying to persuade some of my partners to hold on to perceived fundamental principles that had made the firm professional, prosperous and collegial for two centuries on Wall Street. These certain professional principles were as immutable to me as principles of physics, mathematics or flight. This meant, I would argue, that the firm should not succumb to the current contagious temptation to become simply a bottom-line business. These exhortations were met with a variety of responses, many hostile and derisive.

Now I was convinced that the new managers, together with their supporters, were deeply business-oriented, rather than professionally oriented, and were in no mood to countenance opposition by deed or word. As far as they were concerned, the debate was over and their plan to "modernize" the firm along business lines was to be put into effect.

These managers clearly told me, in different ways, that they were mandated to re-direct the course of the firm and if I didn't like it I could get out. The nature and function of a law firm, they felt, was no different from an automobile company or a fish market. So-called professionalism was, they said, a cover for Dickensian inefficiency; professional values that had guided the partnership since 1818 were "old-fashioned" and, in today's world, "irrelevant." The law profession must be sold.

The managers at the 5:00 p.m. meeting surrounded me at a conference room table piled high with computer printouts and financial reports. The atmosphere was leaden and somewhat sullen. They then proceeded to reiterate, in various degrees of heat, each interrupting the other, why my concepts were outmoded, unscientific, wasteful, and no longer to be tolerated.

All law firms that were going to "survive," they said, were becoming businesses, run like businesses, managed on a day-by-day basis by non-lawyer administrator-accountants. Partners who would not toe the line, would be dealt with in no uncertain terms.

I remember, in some shock, the intensity of the attack as I summarized my case for lawyers retaining professional independence and preserving trust and confidence among partners and between lawyer and client. A manager across from me yawned, over and over, as if to punctuate the absurdity of my remarks.

In this fashion the meeting continued for two hours, as the shadows lengthened. Looking at their faces I had the queasy feeling I was going to be fired, there on the spot. I recall thinking, as the heated session ground on, that the partners who greeted me that Fall day 27 years before would not have gone along with these plans to so radically change the direction of the firm.

Pejorative language rose to greater heights and I felt now the axe would fall. The long knives were out. Then suddenly in a darkening room, there was silence. The managers looked at each other as if frustrated by their task, and said, in effect, well, (as if on cue) this is a sad sack of a situation; we can't resolve it tonight, we will, they said ominously, have to meet again.

The first confrontation was over. When I arrived home, my wife Alexandra met me at the door. "My God," she said, "what happened to you?"

On Thursday, March 25, I distributed to lawyers within the firm a memorandum entitled, "Voyage of a Law Firm." This paper had been composed the previous Sunday, March 21 for submission to the five managers at the meeting with them on March 23. At the time I felt it might be inappropriate, in view of what the managers said, to give them, at that point, "another paper."

The memorandum outlined, in simple terms, my view that a law firm is a professional voyage necessitating cooperation and trust among all the associates and partners. It sought to show how these factors had operated within the firm's Litigation Group, and consequences in terms of profit and success. There was reference in one paragraph on page two to the agreement of the partners of the firm that a partner's financial reward would be in part measured by the extent he had enhanced the professional work and reputation of his partners. This paper, deemed by the angry new managers the "outrageous Voyage memo," was to cause a stir within the firm.

Pertinent portions of this still controversial memorandum are:

*Voyage of the Law Partnership*

"A Law Partnership experience is a peculiar voyage. If you only take a snapshot of the ship and its crew you miss the true flavor — the essential quality and contributions of its component membership, past services, current contributions and the intangible foundation stones laid down for future profits and success.

"Most partners devote more than 30 years, as partners, to their firm — half of their life and virtually all of their time.

"A good law firm is a daring voyage in heavy seas. The rewards of the trip (and the disappointments) are shared. Last week a distinguished law firm simply 'dissolved' after 60 years. Many have fragmented on rocky shoals — in some instances because the partners themselves failed to support each other and took a course of non-cooperation (also known as narcissistic personality dysfunction). Where there is no vision, partnerships perish.

"It is not unnatural for each partner to have his own perception and perspective of individual contribution to the firm. Nor is it unnatural for a partner to obtain comfort from defining 'contribution to the firm' in terms perceived as most favorable to that partner. The business-getters talk of the clients brought in, single-handedly. The account supervisors talk of their incredible billable time. The administative partners tell of their leadership. The accountant partners emphasize their genius with the budget, else expenses would rise to meet income. The youngest partners stress uncanny legal successes and deplore larger shares enjoyed by older partners who were once young and had the same thoughts. Jack Kennedy was right, after all: Life is unfair.

"Our partnership agreement has been a rhetorical landmark for over 30 years. A measure of a partner's remuneration, so the agreement reads, is the extent to which he enhances the professional work and reputation of his partners. Have we always adhered to this resolution? If in reality we have not and do not wish to follow this touchstone we should consider taking the language out.

* * *

"Whatever success [at the firm in the trial department] has been achieved is due to the hard work, training and skill of a closely-knit litigation team of men and women developed over a quarter of a century."

At 4:30 p.m. on Friday, March 26, my secretary was startled by the appearance at the entrance of my office of one of the managers, who shouted at me to come into his office at once. There, gathered by appearance and by conference call, were the five new managers.

They declared that my "Voyage" memorandum was a breach of the most "sacred" bonds of a law partnership—telling "associate" lawyers (not partners) about the collegiality clause in the firm agreement. I was then handed a letter from the managers demanding that I resign or the matter would be taken up with the firm as a whole at a meeting set for the following Monday, March 29. I asked them to reconsider. The managers said no. I then said I would think about it over the weekend and let them know on Monday.

Back in my office I found my secretary, Ann Lauria, pale and upset. I told her what had happened so far as I understood it myself. Then I asked her to give me the telephone number of Whitney North Seymour, Sr., who had been a sympathetic friend, if not mentor, for over 25 years. Mr. Seymour, a senior partner of another large Wall Street firm, listened to my recitation and then said, "Well, what you've just described is endemic in the law firms today. The new managers equate you with the old guard—and you have to go." Then he paused. "But I'll tell you what my advice is, Peter. Go home and talk it over with your real partner, Alexandra. After the weekend is over, you'll know what to do."

For the next two days I talked with Alexandra and a number of friends and advisors, including many of my partners at the firm. By Sunday evening, my decision made, I wrote a letter of resignation for delivery Monday at the firm meeting. The die was cast and we were comfortable with the resolution.

On Monday morning, my counsellor, former Federal judge Harold R. Tyler, Jr., came to my office to convey for me to the managers my decision to resign. After his visit with them, he returned to my office and said, peering out my window overlooking the old Trinity Church graveyard, "After talking with some of the managers," he said, drawing on his pipe, "I want you to know that you are damn well making the right decision."

The firm meeting that day was set for 12:15 p.m. in the firm's largest conference room. The partners sat around one large rectangular table for the lunch meeting. Like some brooding omnipresence in the sky, the ceiling of the room was wired to bring in the voices and audience of partners in Washington, D.C. and Palm Beach. I brought originally signed duplicates of my letter of resignation, to which I attached the alleged catalyst memorandum, "Voyage of the Law Partnership."

Before the shrimp cocktail was consumed, I got up to make my final statement. I then went around the table, shook each partner's hand, gave him my resignation letter which in writing said what I had just expressed to the firm orally. Having completed the rounds, I waved goodbye and exited out the French doors. The ordeal was over. I had no plans. It would be a matter of starting over, but I'd discuss that with Alexandra at lunch.

RESIGNATION LETTER

*{Letterhead of Cadwalader, Wickersham & Taft}*

March 29, 1982

TO ALL MY PARTNERS:

I have now decided what to do with my future professional life. Practicing law at Cadwalader for 26 years has been a stimulating and rewarding experience.

Recently new interpretations of our partnership agreement have come in vogue at this firm. I believe the current management committee is on the wrong course. Quality, excellence, collegiality and grace are not being given sufficient support. These four standards have in the past elevated Cadwalader over 190 years to international recognition for high service to clients, to the Bar and the community. They are now evidently being abandoned. Efforts by some partners to stem this rising tide have met with no success.

Therefore, with regret, I resign from the firm on terms agreed upon with the management committee, effective as of this moment. I wish you well. There is no turning back. I must leave now. I have miles to go in life and in private practice.

Goodbye.

Sincerely,

(signed)

Peter Megargee Brown

"Whether my observations be disproved or supported, I shall be equally satisfied. *Truth is the prize.* There is at least this consolation, that all the competitors may share equally the good attained."

—Sir Dominic Corrigan, in 1829

# *About the Author*

PETER MEGARGEE BROWN practices law in New York City; Yale College, Class of 1944; Yale Law School, 1948; Past President, Federal Bar Council; Special Assistant, New York State Attorney General and Assistant Counsel, New York State Crime Commission, 1951–53 under John Marshall Harlan; Assistant United States Attorney in charge of Federal Waterfront Prosecution, 1953–56 under Judge J. Edward Lumbard; Former Partner and head of Litigation, Cadwalader, Wickersham & Taft; Fellow, American College of Trial Lawyers; partner, Brown & Seymour, Counsellors-at-Law.

*Other books by the author*

The Art of Questioning
Flights of Memory

# *Select Bibliography*

ADAMS, HENRY. *The Education of Henry Adams.* (Boston: Houghton Mifflin, 1918).

ARISTOTLE. *Ethics.* Translated by J. A. K. Thomson. Revised by Hugh Tredennick, Penguin Books; Great Britain, 1987.

*The Politics.* Translated by T. A. Sinclair. Revised by Trevor J. Saunders. Penguin Books; Great Britain, 1981.

ARMSTRONG, SCOTT AND WOODWARD, BOB. *The Brethren.* Simon & Schuster; New York, 1979.

ASSOCIATION OF THE BAR OF THE CITY OF NEW YORK. *The Benjamin N. Cardozo Memorial Lectures,* Volumes I and II. Matthew Bender; New York, 1970.

AUCHINCLOSS, LOUIS. *Diary of a Yuppie.* Houghton Mifflin Company; Boston, 1986.

BACON, FRANCIS. *The Essays.* Edited by John Pitcher, Penguin Books; Great Britain, 1985.

BARNARD, ELLSWORTH. *Wendell Willkie, Fighter for Freedom.* Northern Michigan University Press; Marquette, Michigan, 1966.

BASLER, ROY P., EDITOR; DUNLAP, LLOYD A. AND PRATT, MARION DOLORES, ASSISTANT EDITORS. *The Collected Works of Abraham Lincoln, Volumes I–VIII.* Rutgers University Press; New Brunswick, New Jersey.

BENDER, THOMAS. *New York Intellect.* Alfred A. Knopf; New York, 1987.

BEVERIDGE, ALBERT J. *The Life of John Marshall, Volumes I–IV.* Houghton Mifflin Company; Boston and New York, 1919.

BOSWELL, JAMES. *The Life of Samuel Johnson, LL.D., Volumes I–III.* Swan Sonnenschein & Co., Ltd.; London, 1900.

BOWEN, CATHERINE DRINKER. *Miracle at Philadelphia.* Little, Brown and Company; Boston and Toronto, 1966.

*Yankee from Olympus, Justice Holmes and His Family.* Little, Brown and Company; Boston, 1944.

BRANDT, CLARE. *An American Aristocracy: The Livingstons*. Doubleday and Company, Inc.; New York, 1986.

BROWN, PETER MEGARGEE. *The Art of Questioning*. Macmillan Publishing Company; New York, 1987. *Flights of Memory — Days Before Yesterday — A Memoir.* Benchmark Press, 1989.

BROWNLEE, DAVID B. *The Law Courts, The Architecture of George Edmund Street*. The Architectural History Foundation and the Massachusetts Institute of Technology Press; 1984.

BUCKLEY, WILLIAM F. JR. *On the Firing Line, The Public Life of Our Public Figures*. Random House, 1989.

CARLYLE, THOMAS. *The French Revolution*. Richard Clay and Sons, Limited; London.

CHAMBERS, WHITTAKER. *Witness*. Random House, Inc.; New York, 1952.

CICERO. *On the Good Life.* Translated by Michael Grant. Penguin Books; Great Britain, 1971.

COMMONER, BARRY. *The Closing Circle.* (New York: Knopf, 1971).

COOKE, ALASTAIR. *A Generation on Trial: U.S.A. v. Alger Hiss.* Alfred A. Knopf; New York, 1952.

CROZIER, MICHEL. *The Trouble with America*. Translated by Peter Heinegg. University of California Press; Berkeley, 1984.

DEWEY, JOHN. *Creative Intelligence.* (New York: Holt, 1917).

DUBOS, RENE. *Louis Pasteur — Free Lance of Science.* Little, Brown, 1950.

*So Human an Animal.* Charles Scribner's Sons. New York, 1968.

*Reason Awakd! Science for Man.* (New York: Columbia University Press, 1970).

*Mirage of Health.* (New York: Harper & Row, 1959).

*Man Adapting.* (New Haven, Conn., Yale University Press, 1965).

*The White Plague* (with Jean DuBos).

*The Dreams of Reason.*

*Unseen World.*
*Man, Medicine and Environment.*
*A God Within.*
*Beast or Angel.*
*The Wooing of Earth.*
*Celebrations of Life* (New York: McGraw-Hill Book Company, 1982).

DURRELL, LAWRENCE. *Spirit of Place.* (New York: Dutton, 1969).

ELLUL, JACQUES. *The Technological Society,* translated by John Wilkinson (New York: Knopf, 1965).

FLEXNER, JAMES THOMAS. *George Washington, The Forge of Experience (1732–1775).* Little, Brown and Company; Boston and Toronto, 1965.
*George Washington and the New Nation (1783 – 1793).* Little, Brown and Company; Boston and Toronto, 1969.

FRANK, BARBARA AND JEROME. *Not Guilty.* Doubleday & Company, Inc.; Garden City, New York, 1957.

FRANKEL, MARVIN E. *Partisan Justice.* Hill and Wang; New York, 1978.

GALBRAITH, JOHN KENNETH. *The Affluent Society.* (Boston: Houghton Mifflin, 1958).

GARDNER, JOHN W. *Excellence.* Harper & Row; New York, 1961.

GIBBON, EDWARD. *The Decline and Fall of the Roman Empire.* Penguin Books; New York, 1980.

GOYTISOLO, JUAN. *Landscapes After the Battle.* Translated by Helen Lane. Seaver Books; New York, 1982.

HALBERSTAM, DAVID. *The Best and the Brightest.* Random House; New York, 1969.

HAND, LEARNED. *The Spirit of Liberty.* Edited by Irving Dilliard. Alfred A. Knopf; New York, 1952.

HARBAUGH, WILLIAM H. *Lawyer's Lawyer, The Life of John W. Davis.* Oxford University Press; New York, 1973.

HELLMAN, GEORGE S. *Benjamin N. Cardozo, American Judge.* Whittlesey House, McGraw-Hill; New York, 1941.

HERNDON, WILLIAM H. AND WEIK, JESSE W. *Herndon's Life of Lincoln.* Da Capo Press, Inc.; New York, 1942.

HILL, FREDERICK TREVOR. *Lincoln the Lawyer.* The Century Company; New York, 1906.

HIRSCH, E. D. *Cultural Literacy.* Houghton Mifflin (1987).

HIRSCH, H. N. *The Enigma of Felix Frankfurter.* Basic Books, Inc.; New York, 1981.

HOLLANDER, BARNETT. *The English Bar: A Priesthood.* Bowes and Bowes; London, 1964.

HOLMES, OLIVER WENDELL. *The Complete Poetical Works of Oliver Wendell Holmes.* Houghton, Mifflin and Company; Boston and New York, 1850.

*The Poetical Works of Oliver Wendell Holmes.* George Rutledge and Sons, Ltd.; London, 1896.

HOLMES, OLIVER WENDELL JR. *The Common Law.* Macmillan and Co.; London, 1882.

HORNE, ALISTAIR. *Harold Macmillan, Volume I: 1894 – 1956.* American Edition. Viking Penguin, 1989.

ISAACSON, WALTER & THOMAS EVAN. *The Wise Men.* Simon & Schuster; New York, 1986.

JAMES, WILLIAM. *The Will to Believe.* (New York: Longmans Green, 1907).

JAY, ANTONY AND LYNN, JONATHAN. *The Complete "Yes Minister."* British Broadcasting Corporation; London, 1984.

JOHNSON, PAUL. *Modern Times.* Harper & Row; New York, 1983.

KAHN, HERMAN AND ANTHONY WIENER. *The Year 2000: The Framework for Speculation on the Next 33 Years.* (New York: Macmillan, 1968).

KISSINGER, HENRY. *White House Years.* Little, Brown and Company; Boston and Toronto, 1979.

KNOX, JOHN C. *Order in the Court.* Charles Scribner's Sons; New York, 1943.

LINDSAY, JOHN V. *The City.* W. W. Norton & Company; New York, 1970.

MACHIAVELLI, NICCOLÒ. *The Prince.* Prelude, by Benito Mussolini. The Folio Society. London, 1970.

MACKENZIE, JOHN P. *The Appearance of Justice.* Charles Scribner's Sons; New York, 1974.

MACNEIL, ROBERT. *Wordstruck, A Memoir.* Viking Penguin, 1989.

MCCULLOUGH, DAVID. *Mornings on Horseback.* Simon and Schuster; New York, 1981.

MANCHESTER, WILLIAM. *The Glory and the Dream.* Bantam Books; Toronto, New York, London, 1973.

*The Last Lion: Winston Spencer Churchill.*

*The Lonely Years. Visions of Glory: 1874 – 1932.* Little, Brown and Company; Boston-Toronto, 1983.

MAYER, MARTIN. *Emory Buckner.* Harper & Row; New York, 1968.

MITGANG, HERBERT, EDITOR. *Lincoln As They Saw Him.* Rinehart and Company, Inc.; New York and Toronto, 1956.

MORRIS, RICHARD B. *Alexander Hamilton and the Founding of the Nation.* The Dial Press; New York, 1957.

MOYNIHAN, DANIEL PATRICK. *Loyalties.* Harcourt Brace Jovanovich; New York, 1984.

MUMFORD, LEWIS. *The Myth of the Machine: Technics and Human Development.* (New York: Harcourt, Brace & World, 1967).

*The Myth of the Machine: The Pentagon of Power.* (New York: Harcourt, Brace & Jovanovich, 1970).

MURPHY, BRUCE ALLEN. *The Brandeis/Frankfurter Connection.* Anchor Press/Doubleday & Company, Inc.; New York, 1983.

NELSON, MARCIA. *The Remarkable Hands, An Affectionate Portrait.* Foundation of the Federal Bar Council; New York, 1983.

PAINE, THOMAS. *Common Sense.* Edited by Isaac Kramnick. Penguin Books; Great Britain, 1976. First published 1776.

PAULSON, RONALD. *Representations of Revolution 1789 – 1820.* Yale University Press; New Haven and London, 1983.

PETERS, THOMAS J. AND WATERMAN, ROBERT H. JR. *In Search of Excellence.* Harper & Row; New York, 1982.

PLATO. *The Last Days of Socrates.* Translated by Hugh Tredennick. Penguin Books; Great Britain, 1976.

POSNER, RICHARD A. *Law and Literature—A Misunderstood Relation.* Harvard University Press, 1988.

POWERS, THOMAS. *The Man Who Kept the Secrets; Richard Helms & the CIA.* Alfred A. Knopf; New York, 1979.

REVERE, RICHARD H. *The True and Scandalous History of Howe & Hummel.* Farrar, Straus and Company; New York, 1947.

ROOT, OREN. *Persons and Persuasions.* W. W. Norton and Company, Inc.; New York, 1974.

SANDBURG, CARL. *Abraham Lincoln, The Prairie Years, Volumes I–II.* Harcourt, Brace and Company; New York, 1926.

*The People, Yes.* (New York: Harcourt, Brace, 1936).

*Abraham Lincoln, The War Years, Volumes I – IV.* Harcourt, Brace and Company; New York, 1936.

SEYMOUR, WHITNEY NORTH JR. *United States Attorney.* William Morrow and Company, Inc.; New York, 1975.

SHAMES, LAURENCE. *The Hunger For More.* Time Books; New York, 1989.

SILVERMAN, KENNETH. *The Life and Times of Cotton Mather.* Harper & Row; New York, 1984.

SMITH, RICHARD NORTON. *Thomas E. Dewey and His Times.* Simon and Schuster; New York, 1982.

STEWART, JAMES B. *The Partners.* Simon and Schuster; New York, 1983.

*The Prosecutors.* Simon and Schuster; New York, 1987.

STEVENS, MARK. *Power of Attorney: The Rise of the Giant Law Firms.* McGraw-Hill Book Company; New York, 1987.

STEVENSON, WILLIAM. *Intrepid's Last Case.* Villard Books; New York, 1983.

TAFT, HENRY W. *A Century and a Half at the New York Bar.* Privately printed; New York, 1938.

TARBELL, IDA M. *The Life of Abraham Lincoln, Volumes I–II.* Lincoln Memorial Association and the S. S. McClure Company; 1895.

TILLICH, PAUL. *The Courage to Be.* (New Haven: Yale University Press, 1952).

TRAIN, ARTHUR. *Tutt and Mr. Tutt.* Charles Scribner's Sons; New York, 1922.

TUTT, EPHRAIM. *Yankee Lawyer.* Charles Scribner's Sons; New York, 1943.

UROFSKY, MELVIN I. *Louis D. Brandeis and the Progressive Tradition.* Little, Brown and Company; Boston and Toronto, 1981.

VANDERBILT, ARTHUR T. *The Challenge of Law Reform.* Princeton University Press; Princeton, 1955.

WEINBERG, ARTHUR, EDITOR. *Attorney for the Damned.* Simon and Schuster; New York, 1957.

WELLMAN, FRANCIS L. *The Art of Cross-Examination.* The Macmillan Company; New York, 1903.

WHARTON, EDITH. *The House of Mirth.* Charles Scribner's Sons; New York, 1905.

WHITE, THEODORE H. *America in Search of Itself.* Harper & Row; New York, 1982.

WHITEHEAD, ALFRED NORTH. *Science and the Modern World.* (New York: Macmillan, 1925).

WHYTE, WILLIAM H. *The Last Landscape.* (Garden City: Doubleday, 1968).

WILL, GEORGE F. *The Morning After.* The Free Press, Macmillan, Inc.; New York, 1986.

*Statecraft As Soulcraft.* Simon and Schuster; New York, 1983.

WILSON, SIR CHARLES (LORD MORAN). *Churchill.* Houghton Mifflin Company; Boston, 1966.

WINNICK, R. H., EDITOR. *Letters of Archibald MacLeish 1907 to 1982.* Houghton Mifflin Company; Boston, 1983.